International

Traveler's
Weather Guide

By

Meteorologists

TOM   LOFFMAN

and

RANDY   MANN

Weather
P R E S S

Copyright © 1990 by Weather Press

Printed in the United States of America
10 9 8 7 6 5 4 3 2 1

ISBN: 0-941687-02-3

Library of Congress Catalog Card Number: 90-70281

Published by: Weather Press, Sacramento, Calif.

Please address all correspondence to:
Weather Press
P.O. Box 255427, Suite #330
Sacramento, CA 95865

CREDITS

Concept .... Tom Loffman & Randy Mann

Graphics .... Randy Mann & Mark Katzmann

Design & Layout .... Tom Loffman & Randy Mann

Cover Design .... Mary Gauthier

Laser Typesetting .... Randy Mann

Weather Summaries .... Tom Loffman

Data Entry .... Randy Mann & Dave Moulder

Cover Photography .... Tom Loffman

Printing .... Dome Printing, Sacramento, CA.

Weather Records

Comparative Climatic Data
National Climatic Data Center, Asheville, N.C.

Tables of Temperature, Relative Humidity, and Precipitation for the World, World Climatology Branch of the Meteorological Office, London, England

Worldwide Airfield Summaries
USAF (ETAC) Washington, D.C.

INTRODUCTION

When you're on a trip, whether vacation or business, there's no doubt about it - if the weather is "bad" you're going to be miserable. And, you're going to be even more unhappy when you figure out how much money the whole thing cost you. Even if the weather isn't horrible, it can be wet or cold, and that means you have to carry along extra clothing and coverups - more to lug around. Who needs the aggravation?

And yet, every day there are tens of thousands, perhaps millions, of unhappy travelers who found out too late that they "should have been here last month", or next month. For every location on Earth there's a time when the weather is at its best - and its worst. The trick is to find out about the weather before you make your reservations.

Complete, reliable, easy to understand weather information for worldwide travel planning has been hard to find - and has never been gathered together in one convenient package - at least, not until now. The *INTERNATIONAL TRAVELER'S WEATHER GUIDE* was researched and written with the traveler specifically in mind.

This book isn't just a collection of numbers. It's designed so that you can easily locate your destination in the tables, and quickly plan your trip around the weather. The descriptive text has been keep to a minimum. Yet, with it you can easily identify the best times of the year to visit your travel destination - or note the months to avoid.

Not everyone is going to agree on what is meant by the "best" weather. In my definition, "best" time to travel is when the weather will cause you the least inconvenience - when rainfall is infrequent, temperatures are mild, and humidity is as comfortable as possible. The goal is to pick a time to travel when you won't have to lug around a lot of coats, umbrellas, or foul-weather gear. I believe you should be able to enjoy your trip in the best weather conditions possible so you can get the most out of your travel time and expenses.

Explanation of the Tables

The data in the tables was taken from various government publications, both domestic and international. Some of the international data was originally in Metric. It has been converted to English units of measurement. The data has been checked very carefully for accuracy. However, no guarantee can be made for the ultimate reliability of the data.

Average High Temperature

The high temperature of the day occurs, on the average, about 2-4pm in most locations. In general, the average temperature you are likely to experience during the afternoon will be within several degrees of the average high.

Average Low Temperature

The low temperature of the day occurs, on the average, around sunrise, or within an hour of it. On rare occasions a sharp change in airmass will result in cooler temperatures during the day than the night.

Humidity

A descriptive scale for humidity is presented and is based on the average monthly dew point temperature. I decided to present humidity in this way because relative humidity can be confusing (it is relative to the temperature and therefore cannot stand alone as a measure of comfort) and the dew point temperature is not a familiar concept to most people. The scale works as follows:

70+	dew	point	=	very high humidity
60's	dew	point	=	high humidity
50's	dew	poin	=	moderate
40's	dew	point	=	low humidity
<40	dew	point	=	very low humidity

I think you will find that this scale corresponds well with our subjective experience of humidity. It's based on many years of observation and conversation with people in my capacity as a television meteorologist.

Precipitation Days

This column shows the average number of days during the month with precipitation - either rain or snow. This may be more important than the total precipitation amount, since frequent rainy days can cause more travel problems than a few days with heavy but brief rainfall. In the tropics it can rain almost every day, but the duration of rainfall is short - often less than an hour. Then, the rain stops, and it's back to sunshine again. Rainfall in the middle latitudes can last for many hours, and often all day. Therefore, it's difficult to compare the "raininess" of middle latitude and tropical locations by looking at the number of days with rain. However, it's safe to say that for any given location, the fewer the rainy days, the better your odds are of an enjoyable trip.

Precipitation   Inches

This column shows the total amount of rainfall plus melted snowfall likely to accumulate for each month. Refer to the discussion above on Precipitation Days.

Snowfall   Inches

This column shows the average amount of snow that falls during the month. Snowfall totals can vary widely and are quite sensitive to temperature. Much of the information for European stations had to be computed due to gaps in the data base.

Weather   Records

The individual weather records at the bottom of each data page were taken from a variety of sources and are believed to be current. Since weather records are being broken all the time it's possible that some of these records may be out of date even as they are printed. If you spot one that needs updating, please write in with the new record.

Best Time To Travel

The best months to travel are shown in *italics* for your convenience. Please refer to the discussion above for the definition of "best". I hope you will find this feature a useful aid to efficient trip planning.

TOM   LOFFMAN

Sacramento,   California

March,   1990

ABOUT THE AUTHORS

Tom Loffman is the Chief Meteorologist for KOVR-TV, Channel 13, and KFBK Newsradio 1530 in Sacramento, California. He has been presenting the weather on television since 1976.

Tom prepares his own forecast relying on 23 years of experience in meteorology. Tom also adds to his program segments of educational background information about the weather. These segments utilize his years of experience in meteorology, climatology, statistical analysis, and computer programming skills.

Prior to his years in television, he worked for the National Weather Service Division of Climatology in Honolulu, Hawaii.

Tom is a graduate of the University of California, Berkeley, and has also attended U.C.L.A. He is committed to improving the quality of science education and makes frequent appearances at schools where he presents slide shows about the weather.

Tom holds the American Meteorological Society Seal of Approval for television, and has been a member of that organization since 1975. He is presently a member of the AMS Board of Broadcast Meteorology.

In 1987 he wrote and published Sacramento's first weather book called Tom Loffman's Weather Planner - Sacramento Edition. His second book, recently published is called Tom Loffman's Sacramento Weather Guide.

Meteorologist Randy Mann is also a member of the American Meteorological Society. He has a degree in Geography from the California State University, Sacramento. He has also attended the University of California, Davis, and San Francisco State University.

Randy began his career in meteorology in 1978 at KCRA-TV, in Sacramento. He worked as a forecaster, producer, and on-air weathercaster.

Since 1988, he has been self-employed providing complete computer graphics, book typesetting and other desktop publishing services. The entire contents of this book were generated by him using a PC based publishing system and laser printer.

TABLE OF CONTENTS

UNITED STATES WEATHER

INTERNATIONAL   WEATHER

Asia

Beaufort Wind Scale

Australia

New Zealand

South Pacific

Astronomy

Index

U.S. & International Time Zones

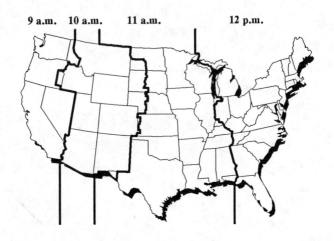

9 a.m. 10 a.m. 11 a.m. 12 p.m.

Time Zones Around The World

	TIME BASED ON 12 P.M. E.S.T.	DIFFERENCE FROM E.S.T.
NEW YORK	12 Noon	0
Acapulco	11 a.m.	- 1
Athens	7 p.m.	+7
Buenos Aires	2 p.m.	+2
Cairo	7 p.m.	+7
Geneva	6 p.m.	+6
Hong Kong	1 a.m.	+13
Johannesburg	7 p.m.	+7
London	5 p.m.	+5
Madrid	6 p.m.	+6
Manila	1 a.m.	+13
Moscow	8 p.m.	+8
Honolulu	7 a.m.	- 5
Paris	6 p.m.	+6
Rio De Janeiro	2 p.m.	+2
Rome	6 p.m.	+6
Sydney	3 a.m.	+15
Tokyo	2 a.m.	+14
Vancouver	9 a.m.	- 3
Vienna	6 p.m.	+6
Wellington	5 a.m.	+17

UNITED   STATES

WEATHER

UNITED STATES
ALASKA & HAWAII

ALASKA

A number of definite statements can be made about Alaska. It is extremely beautiful. There's much to see and do. It can get brutally cold. However, it's not *always* cold. In fact, summertime in Alaska can be warm, and occasionally hot.

First, the humidity - there isn't much of it, so it's not a factor to be concerned about. Temperatures *are* a critical factor in planning your trip to Alaska. The warmest months are, of course, in the summer. June, July, and August are really the only warm ones. In the interior, temperatures can climb to 90 in July. Along the coast summer temperatures remain cool because of the moderating influence of water in the Gulf of Alaska. The **best time to visit** Alaska has to be *June*. Temperatures are nearly at their peak, the days are very long - in some areas 24 hours long, and rainfall is moderate.

Rain increases later in the summer, peaking in August in Fairbanks, and September in Anchorage. By September the days are chilly and the nights cold. By October it feels like winter everywhere in Alaska. And after that, well, it's just cold, but beautiful, as only winter can be in Alaska.

HAWAII

Hawaii is famous for many things, and it's weather is certainly at the top of the list. However, it does rain often - that keeps the flowers growing in abundance, and it *can* rain on your trip. It's important to understand that there is a wet

UNITED STATES
ALASKA & HAWAII

and dry "season" in the islands, and the rainfall varies considerably from one part of each island to the other.

First, the temperatures are generally warm, and it *is* somewhat humid. Winters average about eight degrees cooler than summers. But even in the winter afternoon temperatures near 80 feet just about "perfect".

Rainfall increases in the winter months. The likelihood of several cloudy, showery, humid days, with the Trade Winds absent, increases in October. By November it rains more often, and this type of weather can occur until April. Long stretches of mild, sunny, breezy days can be enjoyed all winter long, however. The pattern of winter rainfall is partly reversed on the Big Island of Hawaii where the moist Trade Winds of summer are forced upward as they encounter the massive volcanic peaks of Mauna Kea, and Mauna Loa. There, it rains more in the summer, but this is an exception in the island chain.

You should also be aware of the fact that areas facing toward the East and Northeast ("Windward" or toward the prevailing Trade Winds) are wetter than the "Leeward" or west and southwest facing shores. Also, the closer to the mountains you get, the wetter it and you will get on any given day. It's also cooler by several degrees as you drive or hike up into the lush, tropical Hawaiian mountains. There really isn't a "bad" month weatherwise in Hawaii, but for the **best combination** of moderate temperature and humidity, infrequent rainfall, and plenty of sunshine, *May* is probably your best bet. Aloha.

UNITED STATES
ALASKA & HAWAII

	JAN	FEB	MAR	APR	MAY	JUN	JUL	AUG	SEP	OCT	NOV	DEC	ANN.
ANCHORAGE, ALASKA - 114 ft.													
Av. High °F	20	27	33	44	55	63	66	64	56	42	28	21	43
Av. Low °F	4	9	15	27	37	46	50	48	40	28	14	5	27
Humidity	V.Lo	V.Lo	V.Lo	V.Lo	V.Lo	Lo	Lo	Lo	Lo	V.Lo	V.Lo	V.Lo	V.Lo
Precip. Days	6	9	8	7	7	8	11	12	13	11	10	11	113
Precip. In.	.8	.8	.6	.6	.6	1.1	2.1	2.3	2.4	1.4	1.0	1.1	14.8
Snowfall In.	11	12	9	6	1	0	0	0	<1	6	10	15	70
FAIRBANKS, ALASKA - 440 ft.													
Av. High °F	-2	9	23	40	59	71	72	66	54	34	12	-2	36
Av. Low °F	-22	-14	-4	17	36	47	50	45	34	17	-6	-19	15
Humidity	V.Lo	V.Lo	V.Lo	V.Lo	V.Lo	Lo	Lo	Lo	V.Lo	V.Lo	V.Lo	V.Lo	V.Lo
Precip. Days	7	7	7	5	6	10	12	12	9	10	9	8	102
Precip. In.	.6	.5	.5	.3	.7	1.4	1.9	2.2	1.1	.7	.7	.6	11.2
Snowfall In.	11	9	8	4	1	0	0	0	1	10	13	12	69
HONOLULU, HAWAII - 38 ft.													
Av. High °F	79	79	80	81	84	86	87	87	87	86	83	80	83
Av. Low °F	65	65	66	68	70	72	73	74	73	72	70	67	70
Humidity	Hi	Hi	Hi	Hi	Hi	Hi	Hi	Hi	Hi	Hi	Hi	Hi	Hi
Precip. Days	10	10	9	9	7	6	8	7	7	9	10	10	102
Precip. In.	4.4	2.5	3.2	1.3	1.0	.3	.6	.7	.7	1.5	3.0	3.7	22.9
Snowfall In.	0	0	0	0	0	0	0	0	0	0	0	0	0
KONA, HAWAII - 18 ft.													
Av. High °F	81	81	81	82	82	83	84	85	85	85	83	82	83
Av. Low °F	65	65	65	66	68	69	69	70	70	69	68	65	67
Humidity	Hi	Hi	Hi	Hi	Hi	Hi	Hi	Hi	Hi	Hi	Hi	Hi	Hi
Precip. Days	10	7	8	7	8	7	8	8	7	6	7	7	90
Precip. In.	3.1	1.7	2.1	1.6	2.3	2.2	2.5	2.4	1.7	1.7	1.8	1.7	24.8
Snowfall In.	0	0	0	0	0	0	0	0	0	0	0	0	0
LAHAINA, HAWAII - 12 ft.													
Av. High °F	81	81	82	83	86	88	88	89	89	88	85	82	85
Av. Low °F	62	62	63	64	66	68	69	69	69	68	66	64	66
Humidity	Hi	Hi	Hi	Hi	Hi	Hi	Hi	Hi	Hi	Hi	Hi	Hi	Hi
Precip. Days	10	12	8	9	5	5	7	6	5	7	9	10	93
Precip. In.	2.8	2.3	2.3	1.3	.5	.1	.2	.6	.3	1.2	1.6	2.7	15.9
Snowfall In.	0	0	0	0	0	0	0	0	0	0	0	0	0

GREATEST U.S. PRECIPITATION IN 1 CALENDAR YEAR: 704.83"
Puu Kukui, Maui, Hawaii - 1982

WIND CHILL

When the wind is blowing the temperature feels colder than it would if the air were still. The combined effects of the wind and temperature create a ''wind chill'' temperature that is lower than a thermometer alone would indicate. The faster the wind, the lower the ''wind chill'' temperature. This lower ''chill'' temperature has the same effect on human skin as the equivalent temperature would in calm air. That is, a ''wind chill'' of minus 10 degrees has the same effect on a person as an actual temperature of minus 10 degrees with no wind. You might call the ''wind chill'' temperature the ''no wind'' equivalent temperature.

Using the table below you can determine the ''wind chill'' by first finding the actual temperature on the left row, then the wind speed along the top column. The ''wind chill'' temperature can be found where the row and column meet in the center. For example, a temperature of 20 degrees with a wind of 10 miles an hour result in a ''wind chill'' of 4 degrees.

WIND SPEED IN MILES PER HOUR

		5	10	15	20	25	30	35	40	45	50
T	35	33	21	16	12	7	5	3	1	1	0
E	30	27	16	11	3	0	-2	-4	-4	-6	-7
M	25	21	9	1	-4	-7	-11	-13	-15	-17	-17
P	20	16	2	-6	-9	-15	-18	-20	-22	-24	-24
E	15	12	-2	-11	-17	-22	-26	-27	-29	-31	-31
R	10	7	-9	-18	-24	-29	-33	-35	-36	-38	-38
A	5	1	-15	-25	-32	-37	-41	-43	-45	-46	-47
T	0	-6	-22	-33	-40	-45	-49	-52	-54	-54	-56
U	-5	-11	-27	-40	-46	-52	-56	-60	-62	-63	-63
R	-10	-15	-31	-45	-52	-58	-63	-67	-69	-70	-70
E	-15	-20	-38	-51	-60	-67	-70	-72	-76	-78	-79
	-20	-26	-45	-60	-68	-75	-78	-83	-87	-87	-88
	-25	-31	-52	-65	-76	-83	-87	-90	-94	-94	-96
	-30	-35	-58	-70	-81	-89	-94	-98	-101	-101	-103
	-35	-41	-64	-78	-88	-96	-101	-105	-107	-108	-110
	-40	-47	-70	-85	-96	-104	-109	-113	-116	-118	-120
	-45	-54	-77	-90	-103	-112	-117	-123	-128	-128	-128

WIND SPEEDS ABOVE 50 MPH HAVE LITTLE ADDITIONAL CHILLING EFFECT

UNITED STATES
THE WEST

The Western United States - often just called "The West" - offers some of the most diverse scenery and weather on earth. The dominating influence on the climate is the vast North Pacific Ocean. It's a cool body of water, and as a result the air masses that sweep over the West contain little of the oppressive humidity that covers the East and Midwest in the summer. But when these waters do give birth to storms in the winter, they are large and powerful, and can bring torrential rainfall and deep snows to the towering mountain ranges that run from Alaska to Mexico.

The immediate Pacific shoreline enjoys a mild, cool climate, thanks to the moderating influence of the ocean. In Washington this shore is damp, rainy, and foggy. Off San Diego it is still damp, but the rains are infrequent, and the temperatures warmer. But the fog is still a problem, especially in the Spring and early Summer. The fogs of San Francisco are world famous.

Farther inland the climate becomes more extreme - that is, days are warmer, nights cooler, and the fog becomes more common in the winter rather than in the summer. If the ocean's cooling sea-breezes are blocked by successive ranges of hills or mountains, the temperatures can soar to well over 100 during the summer months. California often reports the coolest and the hottest spots in the nation on many summer days - Crescent City or Arcata can have a high of 58 with fog, while Death Valley can be 120 under a clear sky and blazing sun. That morning, Truckee, high in the Sierra Nevada north of Lake Tahoe, can report a minimum temperature near freezing - and all on the same day.

UNITED STATES
THE WEST

All of the factors that influence Western weather play their part in this scenario - distance from the ocean, elevation, and the effects of mountains and valleys as they block and channel air masses that attempt to flow over or into them.

In the high, flat plateaus of the Western interior, rainfall becomes scarce, and the only thing that saves several states from being blazing deserts is the cooling effect of elevation.

The Rocky Mountains influence air masses that pass over them in many ways - they intercept moisture from Pacific Storms approaching from the west. They attempt to block cold, Canadian air masses in the winter, diverting them into the Midwest. They catch humidity flowing up over them from the south, southwest or southeast, and generate massive thunderstorms in the summer. And they channel the "Jet Stream" winds that flow over them generating fierce, warming, downslope winds ("Chinook winds") on their eastern front.

Because of the tremendous diversity of Western climates there really is no best time to visit - although as a general rule, *late Spring and early Fall* are **almost ideal**. Winters present the problems of rain, fog, and snow. Summers present problems with heat and thunderstorms in some areas.

For the ideal conditions in any city you will be visiting it's best to study the tables that follow. In the West, there's a climate to satisfy virtually everyone's needs.

UNITED STATES
THE WEST

	JAN	FEB	MAR	APR	MAY	JUN	JUL	AUG	SEP	OCT	NOV	DEC	ANN.
ALBUQUERQUE, NEW MEXICO - 5,311 ft.													
Av. High °F	47	53	59	70	80	90	92	90	83	72	57	48	70
Av. Low °F	24	27	32	41	51	60	65	63	57	45	32	25	44
Humidity	V.Lo	V.Lo	V.Lo	V.Lo	V.Lo	V.Lo	Lo	Med	Lo	V.Lo	V.Lo	V.Lo	V.Lo
Precip. Days	3	4	4	3	4	4	9	9	6	5	3	4	58
Precip. In.	.3	.4	.5	.5	.5	.5	1.4	1.3	.8	.8	.3	.5	7.8
Snowfall In.	2	2	2	1	0	0	0	0	0	0	1	3	11
ASPEN, COLORADO - 7,773 ft.													
Av. High °F	34	37	43	53	64	74	80	78	71	60	45	37	56
Av. Low °F	6	8	15	25	32	38	44	43	36	28	16	9	25
Humidity	V.Lo	V.Lo	V.Lo	V.Lo	V.Lo	V.Lo	Lo	Lo	V.Lo	V.Lo	V.Lo	V.Lo	V.Lo
Precip. Days	8	8	8	8	8	6	7	9	8	7	7	6	90
Precip. In.	1.8	1.8	1.8	1.7	1.6	1.1	1.5	1.6	1.4	1.4	1.4	1.5	18.6
Snowfall In.	27	25	24	11	3	0	0	0	1	5	17	21	134
BOISE, IDAHO - 2,844 ft.													
Av. High °F	37	44	52	61	71	78	91	88	78	65	49	39	63
Av. Low °F	21	27	31	37	44	51	59	57	49	39	31	25	39
Humidity	V.Lo	V.Lo	V.Lo	V.Lo	V.Lo	Lo	Lo	Lo	V.Lo	V.Lo	V.Lo	V.Lo	V.Lo
Precip. Days	12	10	9	8	8	7	2	3	4	6	10	12	91
Precip. In.	1.5	1.2	1.0	1.1	1.3	1.1	.1	.3	.4	.8	1.3	1.4	11.5
Snowfall In.	8	4	2	1	<1	0	0	0	0	<1	2	5	22
DENVER, COLORADO - 5,280 ft.													
Av. High °F	44	46	50	61	70	80	87	86	78	67	53	46	64
Av. Low °F	16	19	24	34	44	52	59	57	48	37	25	19	36
Humidity	V.Lo	V.Lo	V.Lo	V.Lo	V.Lo	Lo	Lo	Lo	V.Lo	V.Lo	V.Lo	V.Lo	V.Lo
Precip. Days	6	6	9	9	10	9	9	8	6	5	5	5	87
Precip. In.	.6	.7	1.2	1.9	2.7	1.9	1.8	1.3	1.1	1.1	.8	.4	15.5
Snowfall In.	8	8	13	10	1	0	0	0	2	4	8	6	60
EUGENE, OREGON - 359 ft.													
Av. High °F	46	52	55	61	68	74	83	81	77	64	53	47	63
Av. Low °F	33	35	37	39	44	49	51	51	47	42	38	36	42
Humidity	V.Lo	V.Lo	V.Lo	Lo	Lo	Lo	Med	Med	Lo	Lo	Lo	V.Lo	Lo
Precip. Days	19	15	17	12	10	7	2	4	5	12	16	19	138
Precip. In.	7.5	4.7	4.4	2.3	2.1	1.3	.3	.6	1.3	4.0	6.5	7.6	42.6
Snowfall In.	5	<1	1	0	0	0	0	0	0	0	<1	1	8

HIGHEST U.S. & NORTH AMERICAN TEMPERATURE: 134°F
Greenland Ranch, Death Valley, California - July 10, 1913

UNITED STATES
THE WEST

	JAN	FEB	MAR	APR	MAY	JUN	JUL	AUG	SEP	OCT	NOV	DEC	ANN.
GRAND CANYON, ARIZONA - 6,971 ft.													
Av. High °F	41	45	50	60	70	81	85	82	77	65	51	43	63
Av. Low °F	20	21	25	31	39	46	54	53	47	37	27	21	35
Humidity	V.Lo	V.Lo	V.Lo	V.Lo	V.Lo	V.Lo	Lo	Lo	V.Lo	V.Lo	V.Lo	V.Lo	V.Lo
Precip. Days	6	6	6	5	3	3	11	11	6	5	5	6	74
Precip. In.	1.5	1.6	1.4	.9	.6	.4	1.9	2.3	1.6	1.2	.9	1.7	16.0
Snowfall In.	15	13	18	9	2	0	0	0	0	2	8	16	83
GREAT FALLS, MONTANA - 3,662 ft.													
Av. High °F	29	36	40	55	65	72	84	82	70	59	43	35	56
Av. Low °F	12	17	21	32	42	50	55	53	45	37	26	18	34
Humidity	V.Lo	V.Lo	V.Lo	V.Lo	V.Lo	Lo	Lo	Lo	V.Lo	V.Lo	V.Lo	V.Lo	V.Lo
Precip. Days	9	8	9	9	11	12	7	7	7	6	7	7	99
Precip. In.	.9	.7	1.0	1.2	2.4	3.1	1.3	1.1	1.2	.7	.8	.7	15.1
Snowfall In.	10	8	10	8	1	<1	0	0	1	3	7	9	57
LAKE TAHOE, CALIFORNIA - 6,230 ft.													
Av. High °F	36	38	43	51	60	68	79	78	70	58	45	39	55
Av. Low °F	17	18	22	27	31	38	43	43	38	32	25	21	30
Humidity	V.Lo	V.Lo	V.Lo	V.Lo	V.Lo	V.Lo	V.Lo	V.Lo	V.Lo	V.Lo	V.Lo	V.Lo	V.Lo
Precip. Days	11	10	10	7	5	3	1	1	3	5	6	9	71
Precip. In.	6.1	5.3	4.1	2.0	1.2	.6	.3	.1	.3	2.1	3.6	5.7	31.4
Snowfall In.	55	47	39	16	5	<1	0	0	<1	3	14	37	216
LAS VEGAS, NEVADA - 2,006 ft.													
Av. High °F	56	61	68	78	88	97	104	102	95	81	66	57	79
Av. Low °F	33	37	42	50	59	67	75	73	65	53	41	34	52
Humidity	V.Lo	V.Lo	V.Lo	V.Lo	V.Lo	V.Lo	V.Lo	Lo	V.Lo	V.Lo	V.Lo	V.Lo	V.Lo
Precip. Days	3	2	3	2	1	1	3	3	2	2	2	2	26
Precip. In.	.5	.3	.3	.3	.1	.1	.4	.5	.3	.2	.4	.4	3.8
Snowfall In.	1	0	0	0	0	0	0	0	0	0	<1	<1	1
LOS ANGELES, CALIFORNIA - 312 ft.													
Av. High °F	65	66	69	71	74	77	83	84	82	77	73	67	74
Av. Low °F	45	47	49	52	55	58	62	62	60	56	51	48	54
Humidity	Lo	Lo	Lo	Lo	Med	Med	Med	Med	Med	Med	Lo	Lo	Med
Precip. Days	6	6	5	4	1	1	1	0	1	2	3	5	35
Precip. In.	3.0	2.8	2.2	1.3	.1	.1	0	0	.2	.3	2.0	2.1	14.1
Snowfall In.	0	0	0	0	0	0	0	0	0	0	0	0	0

LOWEST WESTERN HEMISPHERIC SEA LEVEL PRESSURE: 26.13"
Near Mexico's Yucatan Peninsula in the Eye of Hurricane "Gilbert" - Sept. 13, 1988

UNITED STATES
THE WEST

	JAN	FEB	MAR	APR	MAY	JUN	JUL	AUG	SEP	OCT	NOV	DEC	ANN.
MONTEREY, CALIFORNIA - 15 ft.													
Av. High °F	59	62	62	63	65	67	67	68	72	71	68	63	66
Av. Low °F	41	43	44	45	48	50	51	52	52	50	46	43	47
Humidity	Lo	Lo	Lo	Lo	Lo	Med	Med	Med	Med	Lo	Lo	Lo	Lo
Precip. Days	10	8	8	5	3	1	0	0	1	2	4	9	51
Precip. In.	3.5	2.7	3.0	1.3	.6	.1	0	0	.2	.7	1.6	3.1	16.8
Snowfall In.	0	0	0	0	0	0	0	0	0	0	0	0	0
PALM SPRINGS, CALIFORNIA - 411 ft.													
Av. High °F	68	71	79	87	94	102	108	106	102	91	79	70	88
Av. Low °F	39	43	47	53	58	63	73	71	66	57	47	41	55
Humidity	V.Lo	V.Lo	V.Lo	V.Lo	Lo	Lo	Med	Med	Lo	Lo	V.Lo	V.Lo	Lo
Precip. Days	4	4	3	2	1	1	2	2	2	2	2	5	30
Precip. In.	1.2	1.3	.8	.3	0	0	.3	.3	.4	.3	.5	1.7	7.1
Snowfall In.	0	0	0	0	0	0	0	0	0	0	0	0	0
PHOENIX, ARIZONA - 1,083 ft.													
Av. High °F	65	69	75	84	93	102	105	102	98	88	75	66	85
Av. Low °F	38	41	45	52	60	68	78	76	69	57	45	39	55
Humidity	V.Lo	V.Lo	V.Lo	V.Lo	V.Lo	Lo	Med	Hi	Med	Lo	V.Lo	V.Lo	Lo
Precip. Days	3	4	3	2	1	1	4	5	3	3	2	4	35
Precip. In.	.7	.6	.8	.3	.1	.1	.8	1.2	.7	.5	.5	.8	7.1
Snowfall In.	0	0	0	0	0	0	0	0	0	0	0	0	0
PORTLAND, OREGON - 154 ft.													
Av. High °F	44	50	54	60	67	72	79	78	74	63	52	46	62
Av. Low °F	33	36	37	41	46	52	55	55	51	45	39	35	44
Humidity	V.Lo	V.Lo	V.Lo	Lo	Lo	Med	Med	Med	Med	Lo	Lo	V.Lo	Lo
Precip. Days	19	16	17	14	12	9	4	5	7	13	17	19	152
Precip. In.	5.9	4.1	3.6	2.2	2.1	1.6	.5	.8	1.6	3.6	5.6	6.0	37.6
Snowfall In.	4	1	1	0	0	0	0	0	0	0	<1	1	7
RENO, NEVADA - 4,397 ft.													
Av. High °F	45	51	56	64	72	80	91	89	82	70	56	46	67
Av. Low °F	18	23	25	30	37	43	47	45	39	31	24	20	32
Humidity	V.Lo	V.Lo	V.Lo	V.Lo	V.Lo	V.Lo	Lo	V.Lo	V.Lo	V.Lo	V.Lo	V.Lo	V.Lo
Precip. Days	6	6	6	4	5	3	3	2	2	3	5	6	51
Precip. In.	1.2	.9	.7	.5	.6	.4	.3	.2	.2	.4	.7	1.1	7.2
Snowfall In.	7	5	5	2	1	<1	0	0	0	<1	2	5	27

HIGHEST GLOBAL AVERAGE ANNUAL RAINFALL: 460"
Mt. Waialeale, Kauai, Hawaii

UNITED STATES
THE WEST

	JAN	FEB	MAR	APR	MAY	JUN	JUL	AUG	SEP	OCT	NOV	DEC	ANN.
SACRAMENTO, CALIFORNIA - 17 ft.													
Av. High °F	53	60	64	71	80	87	93	91	87	77	63	53	73
Av. Low °F	38	41	43	45	50	55	58	58	56	50	43	38	48
Humidity	V.Lo	Lo	Lo	Lo	Lo	Med	Med	Med	Med	Lo	Lo	Lo	Lo
Precip. Days	10	9	8	6	3	1	0	0	1	3	7	9	57
Precip. In.	3.7	2.7	2.2	1.5	.5	.1	0	.1	.2	1.0	2.1	3.1	17.2
Snowfall In.	0	0	0	0	0	0	0	0	0	0	0	0	0
SALT LAKE CITY, UTAH - 4,260 ft.													
Av. High °F	37	43	51	62	72	81	93	90	80	66	50	39	64
Av. Low °F	19	23	28	37	44	51	61	59	49	38	28	22	38
Humidity	V.Lo	V.Lo	V.Lo	V.Lo	V.Lo	Lo	Lo	Lo	V.Lo	V.Lo	V.Lo	V.Lo	V.Lo
Precip. Days	10	9	9	10	7	6	4	5	5	6	7	9	87
Precip. In.	1.3	1.2	1.6	2.1	1.5	1.3	.7	.9	.7	1.2	1.3	1.4	15.2
Snowfall In.	13	10	10	5	1	0	0	0	<1	1	6	12	58
SAN DIEGO, CALIFORNIA - 19 ft.													
Av. High °F	64	65	67	68	70	72	76	77	76	73	71	66	72
Av. Low °F	46	48	50	53	57	60	63	64	62	57	51	47	55
Humidity	Lo	Lo	Lo	Med	Med	Med	Hi	Hi	Hi	Med	Lo	Lo	Med
Precip. Days	6	7	7	4	3	1	1	1	1	3	4	6	44
Precip. In.	1.9	1.9	1.5	.7	.3	.1	.1	.1	.1	.4	.9	1.9	9.9
Snowfall In.	0	0	0	0	0	0	0	0	0	0	0	0	0
SAN FRANCISCO, CALIFORNIA - 52 ft.													
Av. High °F	56	59	61	63	65	69	69	70	72	69	64	57	65
Av. Low °F	40	43	44	45	48	50	52	52	52	49	45	42	47
Humidity	Lo	Lo	Lo	Lo	Lo	Med	Med	Med	Med	Med	Lo	Lo	Lo
Precip. Days	11	10	9	6	3	1	0	1	1	4	7	10	63
Precip. In.	4.4	3.0	2.5	1.6	.4	.1	0	0	.2	1.0	2.3	4.0	19.5
Snowfall In.	0	0	0	0	0	0	0	0	0	0	0	0	0
SANTA BARBARA, CALIFORNIA - 120 ft.													
Av. High °F	65	65	68	70	72	73	77	78	78	76	73	67	72
Av. Low °F	39	42	44	47	50	52	56	56	55	50	44	42	45
Humidity	Lo	Lo	Lo	Lo	Lo	Med	Med	Med	Med	Med	Lo	Lo	Lo
Precip. Days	9	9	8	5	1	1	1	1	1	2	4	10	52
Precip. In.	3.6	3.8	3.1	1.2	.3	.1	.1	.1	.1	.6	1.2	4.0	18.2
Snowfall In.	0	0	0	0	0	0	0	0	0	0	0	0	0

HIGHEST U.S. & NORTH AMERICAN SEA LEVEL PRESSURE: 31.74"
Northway, Alaska - January 31, 1989

UNITED STATES
THE WEST

	JAN	FEB	MAR	APR	MAY	JUN	JUL	AUG	SEP	OCT	NOV	DEC	ANN.
SANTA MONICA, CALIFORNIA - 14 ft.													
Av. High °F	65	65	66	68	70	72	75	76	75	72	69	66	70
Av. Low °F	46	47	48	51	54	57	56	60	59	55	51	48	53
Humidity	Lo	Lo	Lo	Lo	Med	Med	Hi	Hi	Med	Med	Lo	Lo	Med
Precip. Days	6	6	5	4	1	1	1	0	1	2	3	5	35
Precip. In.	2.2	2.7	2.5	.7	.1	0	0	0	.2	.3	1.1	3.1	12.9
Snowfall In.	0	0	0	0	0	0	0	0	0	0	0	0	0
SEATTLE, WASHINGTON - 125 ft.													
Av. High °F	45	50	53	59	66	70	76	75	69	62	51	47	60
Av. Low °F	35	37	38	42	47	52	56	55	52	47	40	37	45
Humidity	V.Lo	V.Lo	V.Lo	V.Lo	Lo	Lo	Med	Med	Med	Lo	Lo	V.Lo	Lo
Precip. Days	20	16	17	14	10	9	5	6	8	10	18	20	153
Precip. In.	5.2	3.9	3.2	2.4	1.7	1.6	.9	.9	1.8	3.4	5.3	5.4	35.7
Snowfall In.	4	1	1	0	0	0	0	0	0	0	1	2	9
SPOKANE, WASHINGTON - 2,357 ft.													
Av. High °F	31	39	46	57	67	74	84	82	73	58	42	34	57
Av. Low °F	20	25	29	35	43	49	55	54	47	38	29	24	37
Humidity	V.Lo	V.Lo	V.Lo	V.Lo	V.Lo	Lo	Lo	Lo	Lo	V.Lo	V.Lo	V.Lo	V.Lo
Precip. Days	15	12	11	9	9	8	4	5	6	8	12	16	115
Precip. In.	2.5	1.7	1.5	1.1	1.5	1.4	.4	.6	.8	1.4	2.2	2.4	17.5
Snowfall In.	19	8	5	1	<1	<1	0	0	0	1	5	15	53
YELLOWSTONE NATIONAL PARK, WYOMING - 6,239 ft.													
Av. High °F	26	29	36	48	58	67	77	76	65	52	38	28	50
Av. Low °F	10	10	17	26	34	41	46	45	37	29	20	12	27
Humidity	V.Lo	V.Lo	V.Lo	V.Lo	V.Lo	Lo	Lo	Lo	V.Lo	V.Lo	V.Lo	V.Lo	V.Lo
Precip. Days	13	11	12	10	13	12	10	9	8	9	10	12	129
Precip. In.	1.6	1.3	1.7	1.3	2.0	1.7	1.3	1.2	1.2	1.4	1.4	1.4	17.5
Snowfall In.	30	23	23	10	4	1	0	0	1	7	18	26	143
YOSEMITE NATIONAL PARK, CALIFORNIA - 3,985 ft.													
Av. High °F	47	52	59	67	73	80	90	90	83	71	58	47	68
Av. Low °F	26	28	31	37	43	47	54	52	47	39	31	28	39
Humidity	V.Lo	V.Lo	V.Lo	V.Lo	Lo	Lo	Med	Med	Lo	V.Lo	V.Lo	V.Lo	Lo
Precip. Days	11	10	10	7	5	3	1	1	3	5	6	9	71
Precip. In.	6.4	6.9	5.3	.2	1.4	.5	.2	.1	.4	2.0	3.8	7.4	34.6
Snowfall In.	16	13	16	9	0	0	0	0	0	0	4	15	73

GREATEST U.S. & NORTH AMERICAN SNOWFALL IN ONE MONTH: 390"
Tamarack (Elevation 8,000 ft.), California - January, 1911

EARTHQUAKES

The areas most likely to experience a damaging earthquake are found near the California coast within 50-100 miles of a major crack in the Earth's crust known as the San Andreas Fault. Strong earthquakes have occurred in other areas of the United States, however.

In 1811-12 three major earthquakes shook New Madrid, Missouri. Charleston, South Carolina felt a major quake in 1886. And, a massive jolt caused severe damage in Alaska in 1964.

Earthquakes are measured by two different methods. The first and most famous is the Richter Scale. This scale measures earthquake strength as recorded on a seismograph. Each increase of 1.0 unit on this scale represents an increase in peak strength of 10 times, and an increase of 30 times in total energy released.

The San Francisco earthquake of 1906 measured 8.25 on the Richter Scale. The 1989 quake registered 7.1. A jolt of at least 5.5 is needed to produce significant damage near the "epicenter" of a quake.

The other scale used to measure earthquakes is called the Modified Mercalli Scale. This is a "subjective" scale and measures the amount of damage caused by a quake rather than the strength or energy released. This scale ranges from I (a small quake that causes almost no damage) to a XII (a major quake that causes almost complete destruction).

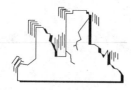

EARTHQUAKES

Earthquake Safety Tips

1. If you're inside a building, stand under a doorway, or get under a table, desk, or bed. Stay away from tall furniture and windows, and do not rush outside.

2. If you're in a crowded building, don't go to be exits, because many people will be doing so. If possible, get under a sturdy object, then choose an exit when it's safe.

3. If you're outside, stay away from high buildings, walls, and power lines. Try to get to an open area.

4. If you're in a car, pull over to the side of the road and stay inside.

Modified Mercalli Intensity Scale

I - Not felt except by very few people under especially favorable conditions.

II - Felt by a few persons at rest, especially on upper floors of buildings.

III - Felt quite noticably indoors, especially on upper floors of buildings, but many people do not recognize as an earthquake.

IV - During the day felt indoors by many, outdoors by few. Sensation like heavy truck striking building.

V - Felt by nearly everyone, many awakened. Disturbances of trees, poles, and other tall objects sometimes noticed.

VI - Felt by all; many frightened and run outdoors. Some heavy furniture moved; few instances of fallen plaster or damaged chimneys. Damage slight.

VII - Everybody runs outdoors. Damage negligible in buildings of good design and construction, slight to moderate in well-built ordinary structures; considerable in poorly built or badly designed structures.

EARTHQUAKES

VIII-Damage slight in designed structures, considerable in ordinary substantial buildings with partial collapse. Great damage in poorly built structures. (Fall of chimneys, factory stacks, columns, monuments, and other vertically oriented features.)

IX - Damage considerable in specially designed structures. Buildings shifted off foundations. Ground cracked conspicuously.

X - Some well-built wooden structures destroyed. Most masonry and frame structures destroyed with foundations. Broad fissures in ground.

XI - Few, if any (masonry) structures remain standing. Bridges destroyed. Broad fissures in ground.

XII- Damage total. Waves seen on ground surfaces. Objects thrown upward into the air.

Source: U.S. Coast and Geodetic Survey.

Richter Magnitudes

Less than 2.5 - Generally not felt, but recorded. Estimated 900,000 per year.

2.5 to 5.4 - Often felt, but only minor damage detected. Estimated 30,000 per year.

5.5 to 6.0 - Slight damage to structures. Estimated 500 per year.

6.1 to 6.9 - Can be destructive in populous regions. Estimated 100 per year.

7.0 to 7.9 - Major earthquakes. Inflict serious damage. Estimated 20 per year.

8.0 or Greater - Great earthquakes. Produce total destruction to communities near epicenter. One every 5 to 10 years.

UNITED STATES
MIDWEST & PLAINS

If you like "wild" weather, you'll like it in the Midwest. Wild means - hot one day, cold the next. It means, very dry one month, and very wet the next, and in no particular order. It means tornadoes, hurricanes (and what's left of them), bitter cold, sweltering heat, and of course lots of thunderstorms. Why does this all occur in the Midwest - at least more of it than in other parts of the country?

First of all, the Midwest is in the middle - that is, away from the oceans. Any body of water modifies and "smoothes out" the climate of nearby land masses. An ocean, for example, will act to keep adjacent land cooler in the summer and warmer in the winter than it would be otherwise. And since the Midwest is by definition away from the ocean, it's climate tends to be rather "un-modified" - not "smoothed out". This area enjoys, or rather "gets", the full brunt of cold Canadian air masses in the winter, and warm, humid air masses off the Gulf of Mexico in the summer. Often these two very different air masses clash, and the result is a variety of strong, and often disagreeable weather - primarily major storms.

The newest term for large storm systems that appear to cover several Midwest states all at the same time is "Mesoscale Convective Complex" - in other words, masses of large thunderstorms all joined together to bring their destructive fury down on large numbers of people and places all at the same time. And all of this thanks to the clash of the wildly different air masses just described.

UNITED STATES
MIDWEST & PLAINS

Some Midwestern cities are near large bodies of water (the Great Lakes), and their climates are modified by these expanses of fresh water. Milwaukee, Chicago, and Detroit are the biggest of these cities, but the lakes are surrounded by smaller cities and towns, all enjoying this modified climate.

The farther north you go in the Midwest the closer to Canada you get, and the cooler and less humid the climate. The coldest temperatures in the country often can be found in North Dakota and Minnesota in the Winter.

A trip to the south toward Texas and Louisiana brings you closer to the warm waters of the Gulf, and the milder the climate becomes - at least in terms of temperature. Humidities increase, and so does the rainfall.

Tornado "season" in the Midwest starts before winter is over in the states near the Gulf, and progresses slowly toward the north reaching the Great Lakes states by early summer.

The best overall combination of moderate temperature and humidity, infrequent rainfall and thunderstorms, and lack of cold "waves" can be found in late summer or early fall - *September* is probably the **ideal month to visit** the Midwest.

UNITED STATES
MIDWEST & PLAINS

	JAN	FEB	MAR	APR	MAY	JUN	JUL	AUG	SEP	OCT	NOV	DEC	ANN.
BISMARCK, NORTH DAKOTA - 1,647 ft.													
Av. High °F	19	25	35	55	67	76	84	84	71	60	39	26	54
Av. Low °F	-3	2	15	31	42	52	57	55	44	33	18	5	29
Humidity	V.Lo	V.Lo	V.Lo	V.Lo	V.Lo	Med	Med	Med	Lo	V.Lo	V.Lo	V.Lo	V.Lo
Precip. Days	8	7	8	8	10	12	9	8	7	5	6	8	96
Precip. In.	.5	.4	.7	1.4	2.2	3.6	2.2	2.0	1.3	.8	.6	.5	16.2
Snowfall In.	7	6	8	4	1	0	0	0	<1	1	5	6	38
CHICAGO, ILLINOIS - 823 ft.													
Av. High °F	31	34	45	59	70	79	83	82	75	66	48	35	59
Av. Low °F	15	18	27	38	47	57	61	60	52	42	30	19	39
Humidity	V.Lo	V.Lo	V.Lo	V.Lo	Lo	Med	Hi	Hi	Med	Lo	V.Lo	V.Lo	V.Lo
Precip. Days	11	10	13	12	11	11	10	8	10	9	10	11	126
Precip. In.	1.7	1.3	2.5	3.4	3.4	4.2	3.5	2.7	3.0	2.3	2.1	1.6	31.7
Snowfall In.	10	8	8	2	<1	0	0	0	0	<1	2	8	38
CINCINNATI, OHIO - 761 ft.													
Av. High °F	40	43	52	66	75	84	87	86	80	69	53	42	65
Av. Low °F	24	26	34	45	54	63	66	64	57	47	36	27	45
Humidity	V.Lo	V.Lo	V.Lo	V.Lo	Med	Hi	Hi	Hi	Med	Lo	V.Lo	V.Lo	Lo
Precip. Days	12	11	13	12	12	13	10	9	9	9	10	11	131
Precip. In.	3.4	2.9	4.1	3.8	4.0	3.9	4.0	3.0	2.7	2.2	3.1	2.9	40.0
Snowfall In.	5	4	3	1	0	0	0	0	0	<1	2	4	19
CLEVELAND, OHIO - 777 ft.													
Av. High °F	33	35	44	58	68	78	82	80	74	64	49	36	59
Av. Low °F	20	21	28	39	48	58	61	60	54	44	34	24	41
Humidity	V.Lo	V.Lo	V.Lo	V.Lo	Lo	Med	Hi	Hi	Med	Lo	V.Lo	V.Lo	Lo
Precip. Days	16	15	16	14	13	11	10	9	10	10	15	16	155
Precip. In.	2.5	2.2	3.0	3.5	3.5	3.3	3.4	3.0	2.8	2.6	2.8	2.4	35.0
Snowfall In.	11	11	10	2	<1	0	0	0	0	1	6	11	52
COLUMBUS, OHIO - 812 ft.													
Av. High °F	36	39	49	63	73	82	85	84	78	66	51	39	62
Av. Low °F	20	21	29	40	49	59	62	60	53	42	32	23	41
Humidity	V.Lo	V.Lo	V.Lo	Lo	Med	Med	Hi	Hi	Med	Lo	V.Lo	V.Lo	Lo
Precip. Days	13	12	14	13	13	11	11	9	9	8	11	12	136
Precip. In.	2.9	2.3	3.4	3.7	4.1	4.1	4.2	2.9	2.4	1.9	2.7	2.4	37.0
Snowfall In.	7	6	5	1	0	0	0	0	0	<1	3	6	28

GREATEST GLOBAL PRECIPITATION IN ONE HOUR: 12.00"
Holt, Missouri - June 22, 1947 (Occurred in 42 minutes)

UNITED STATES
MIDWEST & PLAINS

	JAN	FEB	MAR	APR	MAY	JUN	JUL	AUG	SEP	OCT	NOV	DEC	ANN.
DES MOINES, IOWA - 938 ft.													
Av. High °F	28	33	43	60	71	80	85	83	75	65	46	33	58
Av. Low °F	11	16	25	39	51	61	65	63	54	44	29	17	40
Humidity	V.Lo	V.Lo	V.Lo	V.Lo	Lo	Hi	Hi	Hi	Med	Lo	V.Lo	V.Lo	V.Lo
Precip. Days	7	7	10	10	11	11	9	9	9	7	6	7	103
Precip. In.	1.1	1.1	2.3	3.0	4.2	4.9	3.3	3.3	3.1	2.1	1.4	1.1	30.9
Snowfall In.	8	7	7	2	0	0	0	0	0	<1	3	6	33
DETROIT, MICHIGAN - 619 ft.													
Av. High °F	32	34	43	58	69	79	83	82	74	63	48	35	58
Av. Low °F	19	20	28	39	48	59	63	62	55	45	34	24	41
Humidity	V.Lo	V.Lo	V.Lo	V.Lo	Lo	Med	Hi	Med	Med	Lo	V.Lo	V.Lo	V.Lo
Precip. Days	13	12	13	12	12	11	9	9	9	9	11	13	133
Precip. In.	1.9	1.8	2.3	3.1	3.4	3.1	3.0	3.0	2.3	2.5	2.3	2.2	30.9
Snowfall In.	8	8	5	1	0	0	0	0	0	0	3	7	32
GRAND RAPIDS, MICHIGAN - 784 ft.													
Av. High °F	30	33	42	57	69	79	83	82	74	63	46	34	58
Av. Low °F	16	16	24	36	45	56	60	58	51	41	31	21	38
Humidity	V.Lo	V.Lo	V.Lo	V.Lo	Lo	Med	Med	Med	Med	Lo	V.Lo	V.Lo	V.Lo
Precip. Days	16	12	13	12	11	11	9	9	10	10	14	17	144
Precip. In.	1.9	1.5	2.5	3.4	3.2	3.4	3.1	2.5	3.3	2.6	2.8	2.2	32.4
Snowfall In.	21	12	13	4	0	0	0	0	0	1	9	17	77
GREEN BAY, WISCONSIN - 682 ft.													
Av. High °F	24	27	37	54	66	76	81	79	70	60	42	29	54
Av. Low °F	7	9	20	34	43	53	58	56	48	39	26	13	34
Humidity	V.Lo	V.Lo	V.Lo	V.Lo	Lo	Med	Hi	Med	Med	Lo	V.Lo	V.Lo	V.Lo
Precip. Days	10	8	11	11	12	11	10	10	10	8	9	11	121
Precip. In.	1.1	1.0	1.7	2.7	3.1	3.4	3.1	2.6	3.2	1.9	1.9	1.3	27.0
Snowfall In.	10	9	9	2	<1	0	0	0	0	<1	4	10	44
INDIANAPOLIS, INDIANA - 718 ft.													
Av. High °F	36	39	49	63	73	82	85	84	78	67	51	39	62
Av. Low °F	20	22	30	42	52	61	65	62	55	44	33	23	42
Humidity	V.Lo	V.Lo	V.Lo	Lo	Med	Hi	Hi	Hi	Med	Lo	V.Lo	V.Lo	Lo
Precip. Days	11	10	13	12	12	10	9	8	8	8	10	12	123
Precip. In.	2.8	2.4	3.7	3.9	4.1	4.2	3.7	2.8	2.9	2.5	3.1	2.7	38.8
Snowfall In.	5	5	4	<1	0	0	0	0	0	0	2	5	21

GREATEST U.S. & NORTH AMERICAN SNOWFALL IN ONE SEASON: 1,122"
Mount Rainier-Paradise Ranger Station, Washington - 1971 to 1972

UNITED STATES
MIDWEST & PLAINS

	JAN	FEB	MAR	APR	MAY	JUN	JUL	AUG	SEP	OCT	NOV	DEC	ANN.
KANSAS CITY, MISSOURI - 742 ft.													
Av. High °F	36	42	51	65	74	83	88	87	79	69	53	40	64
Av. Low °F	19	24	32	45	56	65	70	68	59	48	35	24	45
Humidity	V.Lo	V.Lo	V.Lo	Lo	Med	Hi	Hi	Hi	Med	Lo	V.Lo	V.Lo	Lo
Precip. Days	8	7	11	10	10	9	5	8	10	7	6	7	98
Precip. In.	1.2	1.2	2.6	3.5	4.3	5.6	4.4	3.8	4.2	3.2	1.5	1.5	37.0
Snowfall In.	6	4	4	1	0	0	0	0	0	0	1	4	20
MILWAUKEE, WISCONSIN - 672 ft.													
Av. High °F	27	30	39	55	65	75	80	80	72	61	44	32	55
Av. Low °F	11	15	23	35	43	54	59	59	51	41	29	17	36
Humidity	V.Lo	V.Lo	V.Lo	V.Lo	Lo	Med	Hi	Hi	Med	Lo	V.Lo	V.Lo	V.Lo
Precip. Days	11	9	12	12	11	9	11	9	9	8	10	11	123
Precip. In.	1.6	1.1	2.2	2.8	2.9	3.6	3.4	2.7	3.0	2.0	2.0	1.8	29.1
Snowfall In.	12	9	9	2	0	0	0	0	0	<1	3	10	45
MINNEAPOLIS/ST. PAUL, MINNESOTA - 830 ft.													
Av. High °F	21	26	37	56	68	77	82	81	71	61	41	27	54
Av. Low °F	3	7	20	35	46	57	61	60	49	39	24	11	34
Humidity	V.Lo	V.Lo	V.Lo	V.Lo	Lo	Med	Hi	Med	Med	Lo	V.Lo	V.Lo	V.Lo
Precip. Days	9	7	10	10	12	12	10	9	9	8	8	9	113
Precip. In.	.7	.8	1.7	2.0	3.4	3.9	3.7	3.1	2.7	1.8	1.2	.9	25.9
Snowfall In.	9	8	11	3	<1	0	0	0	<1	<1	6	9	46
OKLAHOMA CITY, OKLAHOMA - 1,285 ft.													
Av. High °F	48	53	60	72	79	87	93	93	85	74	61	51	71
Av. Low °F	26	30	37	49	58	67	70	70	61	51	37	29	49
Humidity	V.Lo	V.Lo	V.Lo	Lo	Med	Hi	Hi	Hi	Med	Lo	V.Lo	V.Lo	Lo
Precip. Days	5	6	7	8	10	9	7	6	7	6	5	5	81
Precip. In.	1.1	1.3	2.0	3.5	5.2	4.2	2.7	2.6	3.5	2.6	1.4	1.3	31.4
Snowfall In.	3	2	2	0	0	0	0	0	0	0	<1	2	9
OMAHA, NEBRASKA - 978 ft.													
Av. High °F	33	39	48	64	74	83	89	87	79	69	51	38	63
Av. Low °F	12	17	26	40	52	61	66	64	54	43	29	18	40
Humidity	V.Lo	V.Lo	V.Lo	V.Lo	Lo	Hi	Hi	Hi	Med	Lo	V.Lo	V.Lo	Lo
Precip. Days	7	7	9	9	12	11	9	9	8	6	5	6	98
Precip. In.	.8	1.0	1.6	3.0	4.1	4.9	3.7	4.0	3.3	1.9	1.1	.8	30.2
Snowfall In.	8	7	7	1	<1	0	0	0	0	0	<1	6	32

GREATEST U.S. MEASURED SNOW DEPTH: 451.0"
Tamarack, California - March 11, 1911

UNITED STATES
MIDWEST & PLAINS

	JAN	FEB	MAR	APR	MAY	JUN	JUL	AUG	SEP	OCT	NOV	DEC	ANN.
RAPID CITY, SOUTH DAKOTA - 3,162 ft.													
Av. High °F	34	38	43	57	67	76	86	86	75	64	48	38	59
Av. Low °F	10	14	20	32	43	52	59	57	46	36	23	15	34
Humidity	V.Lo	V.Lo	V.Lo	V.Lo	V.Lo	Med	Med	Med	V.Lo	V.Lo	V.Lo	V.Lo	V.Lo
Precip. Days	7	8	9	10	12	13	9	7	6	4	6	6	97
Precip. In.	.5	.6	1.0	2.1	2.8	3.7	2.1	1.5	1.2	.9	.5	.4	17.1
Snowfall In.	5	6	9	6	1	<1	0	0	<1	2	4	5	39
ST. LOUIS, MISSOURI - 568 ft.													
Av. High °F	40	44	53	67	76	85	88	87	80	70	54	43	66
Av. Low °F	23	26	34	46	56	65	69	67	59	48	36	27	46
Humidity	V.Lo	V.Lo	V.Lo	Lo	Med	Hi	Hi	Hi	Med	Lo	V.Lo	V.Lo	Lo
Precip. Days	8	8	11	11	11	9	9	7	9	8	8	10	109
Precip. In.	1.8	2.1	3.0	3.9	3.9	4.4	3.7	2.9	2.9	2.8	2.5	2.0	35.9
Snowfall In.	4	4	5	0	0	0	0	0	0	0	1	4	18
SPRINGFIELD, ILLINOIS - 588 ft.													
Av. High °F	35	39	49	64	74	83	87	85	79	68	51	38	63
Av. Low °F	19	22	30	43	53	63	66	64	56	45	33	23	43
Humidity	V.Lo	V.Lo	V.Lo	Lo	Lo	Hi	Hi	Hi	Med	Lo	V.Lo	V.Lo	Lo
Precip. Days	9	9	12	12	11	10	9	8	9	7	9	10	115
Precip. In.	1.8	1.8	2.7	4.1	3.5	4.2	3.8	2.7	3.3	3.1	2.1	1.9	35.0
Snowfall In.	5	6	4	1	0	0	0	0	0	0	2	5	22
TULSA, OKLAHOMA - 650 ft.													
Av. High °F	47	52	60	72	79	87	93	93	85	75	61	51	71
Av. Low °F	26	30	37	50	58	67	71	70	62	51	38	30	49
Humidity	V.Lo	V.Lo	V.Lo	Lo	Med	Hi	Hi	Hi	Med	Lo	V.Lo	V.Lo	Lo
Precip. Days	6	7	8	9	10	9	7	7	7	7	6	7	90
Precip. In.	1.4	1.7	2.5	4.2	5.1	4.7	3.5	3.0	4.1	3.2	1.9	1.6	36.9
Snowfall In.	3	2	2	<1	0	0	0	0	0	0	2	1	10
WICHITA, KANSAS - 1,321 ft.													
Av. High °F	41	47	55	68	77	87	92	91	82	71	56	44	68
Av. Low °F	21	25	32	45	55	65	70	68	59	48	34	25	46
Humidity	V.Lo	V.Lo	V.Lo	Lo	Med	Hi	Hi	Hi	Med	Lo	V.Lo	V.Lo	Lo
Precip. Days	5	5	7	8	10	9	8	7	8	6	5	6	84
Precip. In.	.8	1.0	1.8	2.9	3.6	4.5	4.4	3.1	3.7	2.5	1.2	1.1	30.6
Snowfall In.	4	4	3	<1	0	0	0	0	0	<1	1	3	16

GREATEST U.S. SNOWFALL IN A SINGLE STORM: 189.0"
Mt. Shasta Ski Bowl, California - February 13 to 19, 1959

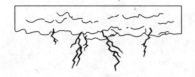 # THUNDERSTORMS & LIGHTNING

Thunderstorms occur in every state. However, they are more severe over mountain areas, the Midwest, the plains, the South, and the East. They are more likely to occur during the spring and summer months, but can be experienced at any time of year. Although thunderstorms present a spectacular light show, they can be very dangerous. Some contain large hail and high winds that often cause property damage and injuries. Therefore, precautionary steps should be taken if you are experiencing a thunderstorm.

Lightning Safety Rules

1. Get inside your home, or an automobile that is non-convertible. If possible, do not use the telephone. Unplug major appliances to prevent possible damage.

2. If you are caught outside, stay in low-lying areas so that you do not project above the immediate environment. Put down golf clubs.

3. Stay away from isolated objects like trees or telephone poles. Do not stand next to metal objects, like wire fences and metal pipes.

4. Get out of, or stay away from, open water.

5. If you're with others, spread out. Lightning may strike you if your hair is standing straight-up. Do not lie flat on the ground. Drop to your knees and bend forward putting your hands on your knees.

Estimating How Far the Thunderstorm is Away From You

If you see lightning, count the number of seconds from the time of the flash until you hear thunder. Divide the number of seconds by five and that's how far away the lightning is in miles.

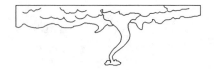 # TORNADOES

Tornadoes are intense low pressure areas with winds in excess of 200 miles per hour. They begin as funnel clouds, a tail-like cloud that hangs from a large thunderstorm. They are classified as tornadoes when the funnel touches the ground. Tornadoes usually form when cold air masses from the north meet warm, moist air masses from the south. They are most likely to form in the late afternoon and early evening, from March to July. However, they have occurred in every month.

Although many parts of the world experience tornadoes, the United States has the highest annual average with more than 700 each year. Every state has experienced a tornado, including Alaska and Hawaii, but the Central Plains (from Texas to Nebraska) may average as many as 4 tornadoes per day during the torando "season".

There are two types of tornado alerts: a *tornado watch*, and a *tornado warning*. A *tornado watch* means that conditions are favorable for the tornado formation. A *tornado warning* means that a tornado has been sighted. If you are in an area that is experiencing a tornado, follow these tips:

1. *If you're at home:* Stay away from windows and outside walls to avoid flying debris. Try to get to a basement, an inside closet, or a bathroom. Never go above the first floor. Don't panic. Monitor conditions with a radio.

2. *If you're in a car:* Get out of the car and take cover inside a building, or in a low-lying area.

3. *If you're in a public building:* Stay away from walls and windows, and try to get to the center of the building. Do not use the elevator. Another area of protection is inside stairwells.

UNITED STATES
THE SOUTH

The climate of the southern states - also known as The South, is warm, humid, and rainy. It can also be quite cloudy, even though it is part of the "Sun Belt". It would be better to call it the "warmth belt" since it is usually warm for the greater part of the year.

The South isn't immune to cold, however. Sub-freezing Canadian air masses sweep through the Midwest and head toward the South during the late fall through the spring months and can drop temperatures into the 20's all the way to the Gulf of Mexico and central Florida.

However, the normal air masses dominating the southern states originate over the Gulf of Mexico or the warm waters of the Gulf Stream. This tepid "stream" starts off the southern tip of Florida, flows up the Atlantic seaboard, and can add quite a lot of moisture to the air masses effecting the southern states. As a result, southern humidities can be quite high, and thunderstorms a daily occurrence.

Because of the high moisture content of the air in the South, rainfall is often torrential, and lightning displays, loud thunder, and even tornadoes are common. But of all the storms of nature, perhaps none is as dramatic as the hurricane - and the South is the primary target for these huge, dramatic, and destructive storms.

The hurricane "season" begins in June and extends through October. No southern state is immune from the threat - either by a direct blow to its coast, or by indirect threat from torrential rainfall, tornadoes, and strong winds as the hurricane

UNITED STATES
THE SOUTH

moves inland and weakens. Most vulnerable to the effect of the hurricane winds and storm surge is the immediate shoreline and any structures or communities along that ocean front.

Many major southern cities are in the "hurricane zone" - Brownsville, Corpus Christi, Galveston, New Orleans, Mobile, Tampa/St. Petersburg, Miami/West Palm Beach, Jacksonville, and Charleston just to name some of the larger cities.

Hurricanes are more likely to effect the South in August and September, when water temperatures in the Gulf and Atlantic are at their warmest. The warmth of the water acts as the fuel that builds that hurricanes' clouds, lowers its pressure, and drives its winds into a swirling fury.

The **best month to visit** the South is *October*. The fall is ideal if you want to avoid the bulk of the tornado and hurricane seasons, and don't care for the heat and humidity of the summer or the chill of winter.

And if you want to avoid winter entirely, you can always spend it in Florida. The coldest weather usually stays north of a line that runs from Tampa to Daytona Beach. If you stay for the winter you'll be called a "snowbird" - if you don't mind that, you'll have a wonderful time hearing about all the cold and snow "up north" while you bask in the sun.

UNITED STATES
THE SOUTH

	JAN	FEB	MAR	APR	MAY	JUN	JUL	AUG	SEP	OCT	NOV	DEC	ANN.
ATLANTA, GEORGIA - 1,054 ft.													
Av. High °F	51	55	61	71	79	85	87	86	81	73	62	53	70
Av. Low °F	33	36	41	51	59	67	69	69	63	52	41	34	51
Humidity	V.Lo	V.Lo	V.Lo	Lo	Med	Hi	Hi	Hi	Hi	Med	Lo	V.Lo	Med
Precip. Days	11	10	12	9	9	10	12	9	7	6	8	10	113
Precip. In.	4.3	4.4	5.8	4.6	3.7	3.8	4.9	3.5	3.2	2.5	3.4	4.2	48.3
Snowfall In.	1	<1	<1	0	0	0	0	0	0	0	0	<1	2
AUSTIN, TEXAS - 597 ft.													
Av. High °F	60	64	71	79	85	92	95	96	89	81	70	63	79
Av. Low °F	39	43	48	58	65	71	74	74	69	59	48	42	57
Humidity	V.Lo	Lo	Lo	Med	Hi	Hi	Hi	Hi	Hi	Med	Lo	Lo	Med
Precip. Days	8	8	7	7	8	6	5	6	7	6	7	7	82
Precip. In.	1.9	3.1	1.9	3.5	4.0	3.1	1.9	2.2	3.7	3.0	2.0	2.2	32.5
Snowfall In.	1	<1	<1	0	0	0	0	0	0	0	0	0	1
BIRMINGHAM, ALABAMA - 620 ft.													
Av. High °F	54	58	65	75	83	88	90	90	85	76	64	56	74
Av. Low °F	34	36	42	51	58	66	70	69	63	51	40	35	51
Humidity	V.Lo	V.Lo	Lo	Lo	Med	Hi	Hi	Hi	Hi	Med	Lo	V.Lo	Med
Precip. Days	11	11	11	9	9	10	13	10	8	6	9	11	118
Precip. In.	4.8	5.3	6.2	4.6	3.6	4.0	5.2	4.3	3.7	2.6	3.7	5.2	53.2
Snowfall In.	1	0	0	0	0	0	0	0	0	0	0	<1	1
CHARLESTON, SOUTH CAROLINA - 9 ft.													
Av. High °F	60	62	68	76	83	88	89	89	85	77	68	61	75
Av. Low °F	37	39	45	53	61	68	71	71	66	55	44	38	54
Humidity	Lo	Lo	Lo	Med	Hi	Hi	V.Hi	V.Hi	Hi	Med	Lo	V.Lo	Med
Precip. Days	10	9	11	7	9	11	14	13	9	6	7	8	114
Precip. In.	2.9	3.3	4.8	3.0	3.8	6.3	8.2	6.4	5.2	3.0	2.1	3.1	52.1
Snowfall In.	<1	<1	<1	0	0	0	0	0	0	0	0	<1	1
CHARLESTON, WEST VIRGINIA - 939 ft.													
Av. High °F	44	46	55	68	77	83	86	84	79	69	56	45	66
Av. Low °F	25	27	34	44	52	61	64	63	56	45	35	27	44
Humidity	V.Lo	V.Lo	V.Lo	Lo	Med	Hi	Hi	Hi	Med	Lo	V.Lo	V.Lo	Lo
Precip. Days	15	14	15	14	13	11	13	10	9	9	12	14	149
Precip. In.	3.4	3.1	4.0	3.3	3.5	3.3	5.0	3.7	2.9	2.5	2.8	3.2	40.7
Snowfall In.	9	8	4	<1	0	0	0	0	0	<1	3	5	29

GREATEST U.S. & NORTH AMERICAN PRECIPITATION IN 24 HOURS: 43.00"
Alvin, Texas - July 25 to 26, 1979

UNITED STATES
THE SOUTH

	JAN	FEB	MAR	APR	MAY	JUN	JUL	AUG	SEP	OCT	NOV	DEC	ANN.
CHARLOTTE, NORTH CAROLINA - 736 ft.													
Av. High °F	52	55	62	73	80	86	88	87	82	73	62	53	71
Av. Low °F	32	33	39	49	57	65	69	68	62	50	40	32	50
Humidity	V.Lo	V.Lo	V.Lo	Lo	Med	Hi	Hi	Hi	Hi	Med	V.Lo	V.Lo	Lo
Precip. Days	10	10	12	9	9	10	12	9	7	7	7	10	112
Precip. In.	3.5	3.8	4.5	3.4	2.9	3.7	4.6	4.0	3.5	2.7	2.7	3.4	42.7
Snowfall In.	2	1	1	0	0	0	0	0	0	0	<1	1	5
DALLAS/FT. WORTH, TEXAS - 512 ft.													
Av. High °F	56	60	67	76	83	91	96	96	89	79	68	59	77
Av. Low °F	34	38	43	54	62	70	74	74	67	56	44	37	54
Humidity	V.Lo	V.Lo	Lo	Med	Hi	Hi	Hi	Hi	Hi	Med	Lo	V.Lo	Med
Precip. Days	7	6	7	9	8	6	5	5	7	6	6	6	78
Precip. In.	1.8	2.4	2.5	4.3	4.5	3.0	1.8	2.3	3.2	2.7	2.0	1.8	32.3
Snowfall In.	1	1	<1	0	0	0	0	0	0	0	<1	<1	3
DAYTONA BEACH, FLORIDA - 31 ft.													
Av. High °F	69	70	75	80	85	88	90	90	87	81	75	70	80
Av. Low °F	48	49	53	59	65	70	72	73	72	65	55	49	61
Humidity	Med	Med	Med	Med	Hi	V.Hi	V.Hi	V.Hi	V.Hi	Hi	Med	Med	Hi
Precip. Days	7	8	8	6	9	13	14	14	13	11	7	7	117
Precip. In.	2.0	2.9	3.4	2.4	2.7	6.6	6.7	6.8	7.1	5.5	2.1	2.0	50.2
Snowfall In.	0	0	0	0	0	0	0	0	0	0	0	0	0
HOUSTON, TEXAS - 41 ft.													
Av. High °F	63	66	72	79	86	91	94	94	90	84	73	66	80
Av. Low °F	42	45	50	59	66	71	73	72	68	58	49	43	58
Humidity	Lo	Lo	Med	Hi	Hi	V.Hi	V.Hi	V.Hi	Hi	Hi	Med	Lo	Hi
Precip. Days	11	6	10	7	9	8	10	10	10	8	8	9	106
Precip. In.	3.6	3.5	2.7	3.5	5.1	4.5	4.1	4.4	4.7	4.1	4.0	4.0	48.2
Snowfall In.	<1	<1	0	0	0	0	0	0	0	0	0	0	<1
JACKSON, MISSISSIPPI - 310 ft.													
Av. High °F	58	62	69	78	85	91	93	93	88	60	69	61	77
Av. Low °F	36	38	43	53	60	68	71	70	64	52	42	37	53
Humidity	Lo	Lo	Lo	Med	Med	Hi	V.Hi	V.Hi	Hi	Med	Lo	V.Lo	Med
Precip. Days	11	9	11	9	9	8	11	11	9	6	8	11	113
Precip. In.	4.5	4.6	5.6	4.7	4.4	3.4	4.3	3.6	3.0	2.2	3.9	5.0	49.2
Snowfall In.	<1	<1	<1	0	0	0	0	0	0	0	0	0	1

LOWEST U.S. & NORTH AMERICAN SEA LEVEL PRESSURE: 26.35"
Matecumbe Key, Florida - September 2, 1935

42

UNITED STATES
THE SOUTH

	JAN	FEB	MAR	APR	MAY	JUN	JUL	AUG	SEP	OCT	NOV	DEC	ANN.

LITTLE ROCK, ARKANSAS - 257 ft.

	JAN	FEB	MAR	APR	MAY	JUN	JUL	AUG	SEP	OCT	NOV	DEC	ANN.
Av. High °F	50	54	62	74	81	89	93	93	86	76	62	52	73
Av. Low °F	29	32	39	50	58	67	70	69	61	49	38	31	49
Humidity	V.Lo	V.Lo	V.Lo	Lo	Hi	Hi	V.Hi	Hi	Hi	Med	Lo	V.Lo	Med
Precip. Days	10	9	11	10	10	8	8	7	7	6	8	9	103
Precip. In.	4.3	4.4	4.9	5.3	5.3	3.5	3.4	3.0	3.6	3.0	3.7	4.1	48.5
Snowfall In.	2	1	1	0	0	0	0	0	0	0	<1	1	5

LOUISVILLE, KENTUCKY - 477 ft.

	JAN	FEB	MAR	APR	MAY	JUN	JUL	AUG	SEP	OCT	NOV	DEC	ANN.
Av. High °F	42	45	54	67	76	84	87	87	81	70	55	44	66
Av. Low °F	25	27	34	45	54	63	66	65	58	46	35	27	45
Humidity	V.Lo	V.Lo	V.Lo	Lo	Med	Hi	Hi	Hi	Med	Lo	V.Lo	V.Lo	Lo
Precip. Days	12	11	13	12	11	10	11	8	8	7	10	11	124
Precip. In.	3.5	3.5	5.0	4.1	4.2	4.1	3.8	3.0	2.9	2.4	3.3	3.3	43.1
Snowfall In.	5	4	4	<1	0	0	0	0	0	<1	1	2	17

MEMPHIS, TENNESSEE - 258 ft.

	JAN	FEB	MAR	APR	MAY	JUN	JUL	AUG	SEP	OCT	NOV	DEC	ANN.
Av. High °F	49	53	61	73	81	89	92	91	84	75	62	52	72
Av. Low °F	32	34	41	52	61	69	72	70	63	51	40	34	52
Humidity	V.Lo	V.Lo	V.Lo	Lo	Med	Hi	Hi	Hi	Hi	Lo	V.Lo	V.Lo	Med
Precip. Days	10	10	11	10	9	8	9	8	7	6	8	10	106
Precip. In.	4.9	4.7	5.1	5.4	4.4	3.5	3.5	3.4	3.0	2.6	3.9	4.7	49.1
Snowfall In.	2	1	1	0	0	0	0	0	0	0	<1	1	5

MIAMI, FLORIDA - 25 ft.

	JAN	FEB	MAR	APR	MAY	JUN	JUL	AUG	SEP	OCT	NOV	DEC	ANN.
Av. High °F	76	77	80	83	85	88	89	90	88	85	80	77	83
Av. Low °F	59	59	63	67	71	74	76	76	75	71	65	60	68
Humidity	Med	Med	Hi	Hi	Hi	V.Hi	V.Hi	V.Hi	V.Hi	Hi	Hi	Med	Hi
Precip. Days	7	6	6	6	10	15	16	17	18	15	8	7	131
Precip. In.	2.2	2.0	2.1	3.6	6.1	9.0	6.9	6.7	8.7	8.2	2.7	1.6	59.8
Snowfall In.	0	0	0	0	0	0	0	0	0	0	0	0	0

NASHVILLE, TENNESSEE - 546 ft.

	JAN	FEB	MAR	APR	MAY	JUN	JUL	AUG	SEP	OCT	NOV	DEC	ANN.
Av. High °F	48	51	59	71	80	88	90	89	84	73	59	50	70
Av. Low °F	29	31	38	49	57	66	69	68	61	49	38	31	49
Humidity	V.Lo	V.Lo	V.Lo	Lo	Med	Hi	Hi	Hi	Hi	Lo	V.Lo	V.Lo	Lo
Precip. Days	11	11	12	11	11	10	10	9	8	7	9	11	120
Precip. In.	4.8	4.4	5.0	4.1	4.1	3.4	3.8	3.2	3.1	2.2	3.5	4.4	46.0
Snowfall In.	3	3	2	<1	0	0	0	0	0	0	1	2	11

LOWEST GLOBAL PRECIPITATION IN ONE YEAR: 0.00"
Bagdad, CA (1913), Greenland Ranch, CA (1929), Iquique, Chile (Nov '45-May '57)

UNITED STATES
THE SOUTH

	JAN	FEB	MAR	APR	MAY	JUN	JUL	AUG	SEP	OCT	NOV	DEC	ANN.
NEW ORLEANS, LOUISIANA - 8 ft.													
Av. High °F	62	65	70	78	85	90	90	91	87	80	70	64	78
Av. Low °F	44	46	51	59	65	71	73	73	70	60	50	45	59
Humidity	Lo	Lo	Med	Med	Hi	V.Hi	V.Hi	V.Hi	V.Hi	Hi	Med	Lo	Hi
Precip. Days	10	9	9	7	8	10	15	13	10	6	7	10	114
Precip. In.	4.5	4.8	5.5	4.2	4.2	4.7	6.7	5.2	5.6	2.3	3.9	5.1	56.8
Snowfall In.	0	0	0	0	0	0	0	0	0	0	0	0	0
ORLANDO, FLORIDA - 108 ft.													
Av. High °F	71	72	76	82	87	89	90	90	88	83	76	72	81
Av. Low °F	50	51	56	61	66	71	73	74	72	66	57	52	62
Humidity	Med	Med	Med	Med	Hi	V.Hi	V.Hi	V.Hi	V.Hi	Hi	Med	Med	Hi
Precip. Days	6	7	8	5	9	14	18	16	14	9	5	6	117
Precip. In.	2.3	2.9	3.5	2.7	2.9	7.1	8.3	6.7	7.2	4.1	1.6	1.9	51.2
Snowfall In.	0	0	0	0	0	0	0	0	0	0	0	0	0
RALEIGH, NORTH CAROLINA - 434 ft.													
Av. High °F	51	53	61	72	79	86	88	87	82	72	62	52	70
Av. Low °F	30	31	37	47	55	63	67	66	60	48	38	31	48
Humidity	V.Lo	V.Lo	V.Lo	Lo	Med	Hi	Hi	Hi	Hi	Med	V.Lo	V.Lo	Lo
Precip. Days	10	10	11	9	10	9	11	10	8	7	8	9	112
Precip. In.	3.2	3.3	3.4	3.1	3.3	3.7	5.1	4.9	3.8	2.8	2.8	3.1	42.5
Snowfall In.	3	2	1	0	0	0	0	0	0	0	<1	1	7
RICHMOND, VIRGINIA - 144 ft.													
Av. High °F	47	50	58	70	78	85	88	87	81	71	61	49	69
Av. Low °F	28	29	36	45	55	63	68	66	59	47	37	29	47
Humidity	V.Lo	V.Lo	V.Lo	Lo	Med	Hi	Hi	Hi	Hi	Lo	V.Lo	V.Lo	Lo
Precip. Days	10	9	11	9	11	10	11	10	8	7	8	9	113
Precip. In.	2.9	3.0	3.4	2.8	3.4	3.5	5.6	5.1	3.6	2.9	3.2	3.2	42.6
Snowfall In.	5	3	3	<1	0	0	0	0	0	0	<1	2	14
TAMPA/ST. PETERSBURG, FLORIDA - 19 ft.													
Av. High °F	71	72	75	82	88	90	90	90	89	84	77	72	82
Av. Low °F	50	52	56	62	67	72	74	74	73	66	56	51	63
Humidity	Med	Med	Med	Hi	Hi	V.Hi	V.Hi	V.Hi	V.Hi	Hi	Hi	Med	Hi
Precip. Days	6	7	7	5	6	12	16	16	13	7	5	6	106
Precip. In.	2.3	2.9	3.9	2.1	2.4	6.5	8.4	8.0	6.4	2.5	1.8	2.2	49.4
Snowfall In.	0	0	0	0	0	0	0	0	0	0	0	0	0

LOWEST GLOBAL PRECIPITATION IN ONE YEAR: 0.00"
Kharga, Egypt (Dec. '57-Mar. '60), Wadi Halfa, Sudan (Jun. '45-Apr. '49)

HURRICANES

A hurricane is an intense storm of tropical origin with sustained winds of at least 74 miles per hour. Hurricanes that effect the U.S. originate in the Atlantic, the Caribbean Sea, and the Eastern North Pacific ocean. These massive storms form over warm, tropical waters, beginning innocently as a group of scattered thunderstorms.

As the storm becomes more "organized" and the winds near the center increase to 75 miles per hour or more, a clear area forms in the center called the "eye". Weather in the eye is generally partly cloudy with light winds.

The "wall" of the eye consists of fierce winds, heavy rain, and often tornadoes. This area is the most intense part of the hurricane. Winds in the "eye wall" can exceed 155 miles per hour in the bigger storms.

The hurricane "season" runs from June through November for the Atlantic and Caribbean. However, almost twice as many hurricanes form in the Eastern North Pacific. The Atlantic/Caribbean hurricanes generally receive more publicity since they effect the heavily populated U.S. coastline from Texas to Florida, then up to Maine.

Since two or more storms can be present at the same time they are given names to avoid confusion. In recent years, female and male names alternate, and the names are different for the Atlantic/Caribbean and the Pacific.

HURRICANES

Category	Central Pressure	Winds (MPH)	. Storm Surge	Property Damage
1	28.94"	74-95	4-5'	Minimal
2	28.50-28.93"	96-110	6-8'	Moderate
3	27.90-28.49"	111-130	9-12'	Extensive
4	27.17-27.89"	131-155	13-18'	Extensive
5	27.16" or Less	156 or More	18.1' or More	Catastrophic

Based on the Saffir/Simpson Damage-Potential Scale

ATLANTIC HURRICANE NAMES
Information Number: 1-900-410-2263*

1990 - Arthur, Bertha, Cesar, Diana, Edouard, Fran, Gustav, Hortense, Isidore, Josephine, Klaus, Lill, Marco, Nana, Omar, Paloma, Rene, Sally, Teddy, Vicky, Wilfred

1991 - Ana, Bob, Claudette, Davis, Erika, Fabian, Grace, Henri, Isabel, Juan, Kate, Larry, Mindy, Nicholas, Odette, Peter, Rose, Sam, Theresa, Victor, Wanda

EASTERN PACIFIC HURRICANE NAMES
Information Number: 1-900-410-6622*

1990 - Alma, Boris, Christina, Douglas, Elida, Fausto, Genevieve, Hernan, Iselle, Julio, Kenna, Lowell, Marie, Norbert, Odile, Polo, Rachel, Simon, Trudy, Vance, Wallis, Xavier, Yolanda, Zeke

1991 - Andres, Blanca, Carlos, Dolores, Enrique, Fefa, Guillermo, Hilda, Ignacio, Jimena, Kevin, Linda, Marty, Nora, Olaf, Pauline, Rick, Sandra, Terry, Vivian, Waldo, Xina, York, Zelda

* Infomation calls are 50 cents first minute, and 35 cents each additional minute.

UNITED STATES
THE EAST

Eastern weather is known for its variety. Unlike western weather, where the climate can change radically from city to city, the weather in the East has definite, memorable, genuine seasons. Summers are warm and humid, falls are colorful, winters are cold with snow, and springs are changeable with everything in bloom - right out of the textbooks.

The East is obviously east of everything else in the country. Since weather "systems" generally move from west to east, almost all storms that start somewhere else in the country, eventually end up somewhere in the East. This includes cold Canadian winter air masses and milder Pacific storms that move all the way across the continent in a matter of days. The East often ends up with rain from "lows" that form in the Gulf of Mexico. Even hurricanes that start far out in the Atlantic can strike the East Coast somewhere between Cape Hatteras and New England.

East Coast weather is strongly influenced by the Gulf Stream, that warm current of tropical, warm water that flows from South Florida, up the Atlantic seaboard, then out into the North Atlantic. Because of the stream's warmth, the East has milder temperatures in the winter than Midwestern states at the same latitude. This same warm water current can add quite a bit of humidity to the air masses that effect the eastern states, and the result can be heavy rainfall in any month. In fact, there really is no dominant "rainy season" in the East.

However, a bit more rain does fall in the summer than the winter because of the added moisture content of the summertime air.

UNITED STATES
THE EAST

The long mountain ranges that separate the Atlantic coastal plain from the Midwest - the Green Mountains and Adirondacks in the North, and the Appalachians farther south - also help to isolate the East to some extent from the extremes of Midwestern air masses and storms. In particular, the mountains interfere with the cross currents of air needed to produce tornadoes, and hence act as a barrier that keeps the number of tornadoes to a minimum from D.C. to New England.

Eastern summer weather can be very warm and humid, especially during July and August. All factors considered, *late May and early June and the month of September* are just about **ideal times** to take a trip to the East. If it's sheer beauty you are looking for, the peak of fall can be enjoyed in October.

If you love to ski, head for New England in the winter. And if you love to see nature at its finest, you might enjoy a visit during spring. So what's wrong with summer? Head for New England and have a great time.

UNITED STATES
THE EAST

	JAN	FEB	MAR	APR	MAY	JUN	JUL	AUG	SEP	OCT	NOV	DEC	ANN.
ALBANY, NEW YORK - 275 ft.													
Av. High °F	30	33	43	58	70	79	84	81	74	63	48	34	58
Av. Low °F	13	14	24	36	46	56	60	58	50	40	31	18	37
Humidity	V.Lo	V.Lo	V.Lo	V.Lo	Lo	Med	Hi	Med	Med	Lo	V.Lo	V.Lo	V.Lo
Precip. Days	13	11	12	12	13	11	11	10	9	9	12	13	136
Precip. In.	2.2	2.1	2.6	2.7	3.3	3.0	3.1	2.9	3.1	2.6	2.8	2.9	33.3
Snowfall In.	15	15	12	3	0	0	0	0	0	<1	4	16	65
ATLANTIC CITY, NEW JERSEY - 64 ft.													
Av. High °F	41	43	51	62	72	81	85	83	77	68	56	44	64
Av. Low °F	24	25	32	41	51	60	65	64	57	46	36	26	44
Humidity	V.Lo	V.Lo	V.Lo	Lo	Med	Hi	Hi	Hi	Med	Lo	V.Lo	V.Lo	Lo
Precip. Days	11	10	11	11	10	9	9	9	8	7	9	9	113
Precip. In.	3.6	3.4	4.3	3.4	3.5	3.4	4.3	4.9	3.0	3.5	4.2	4.0	45.5
Snowfall In.	5	5	3	<1	0	0	0	0	0	0	<1	2	16
BALTIMORE, MARYLAND - 14 ft.													
Av. High °F	42	44	53	65	75	83	87	85	79	68	56	44	65
Av. Low °F	25	26	33	42	53	62	67	65	58	46	36	27	45
Humidity	V.Lo	V.Lo	V.Lo	Lo	Med	Hi	Hi	Hi	Med	Lo	V.Lo	V.Lo	Lo
Precip. Days	10	9	11	11	11	9	9	10	8	7	9	9	113
Precip. In.	2.9	2.8	3.7	3.1	3.6	3.8	4.1	4.2	3.1	2.8	3.1	3.3	40.5
Snowfall In.	5	6	5	<1	0	0	0	0	0	0	1	5	22
BOSTON, MASSACHUSETTS - 124 ft.													
Av. High °F	36	38	45	56	67	77	81	79	72	63	52	39	59
Av. Low °F	23	23	32	41	50	59	65	63	57	48	39	27	44
Humidity	V.Lo	V.Lo	V.Lo	V.Lo	Lo	Med	Hi	Hi	Lo	Med	V.Lo	V.Lo	V.Lo
Precip. Days	12	11	12	11	12	11	9	10	9	9	11	12	129
Precip. In.	3.7	3.5	4.0	3.5	3.5	3.2	2.7	3.5	3.2	3.0	4.5	4.2	42.5
Snowfall In.	12	12	8	1	0	0	0	0	0	0	1	8	42
BUFFALO, NEW YORK - 705 ft.													
Av. High °F	30	31	39	53	64	75	80	78	71	60	46	34	55
Av. Low °F	18	18	25	36	46	56	61	59	52	43	34	22	39
Humidity	V.Lo	V.Lo	V.Lo	V.Lo	Lo	Med	Med	Med	Med	Lo	V.Lo	V.Lo	V.Lo
Precip. Days	20	17	16	14	13	10	10	10	10	11	16	20	167
Precip. In.	2.9	2.5	2.9	3.2	3.0	2.2	2.9	3.5	3.3	3.0	3.7	3.0	36.1
Snowfall In.	22	18	12	3	<1	0	0	0	0	<1	13	22	90

GREATEST GLOBAL RECORDED WIND SPEED: 231 MPH
Mount Washington, New Hampshire - April 12, 1934

UNITED STATES
THE EAST

	JAN	FEB	MAR	APR	MAY	JUN	JUL	AUG	SEP	OCT	NOV	DEC	ANN.

BURLINGTON, VERMONT - 332 ft.

	JAN	FEB	MAR	APR	MAY	JUN	JUL	AUG	SEP	OCT	NOV	DEC	ANN.
Av. High °F	26	28	38	53	66	77	81	78	70	59	44	30	54
Av. Low °F	8	9	20	33	44	54	59	56	49	39	30	15	35
Humidity	V.Lo	V.Lo	V.Lo	V.Lo	Lo	Med	Med	Med	Med	Lo	V.Lo	V.Lo	V.Lo
Precip. Days	14	12	13	12	14	12	12	12	12	11	14	15	153
Precip. In.	1.7	1.7	1.9	2.6	3.0	3.5	3.5	3.7	3.1	2.7	2.9	2.2	32.5
Snowfall In.	18	18	12	4	0	0	0	0	0	<1	7	20	79

CONCORD, NEW HAMPSHIRE - 342 ft.

	JAN	FEB	MAR	APR	MAY	JUN	JUL	AUG	SEP	OCT	NOV	DEC	ANN.
Av. High °F	31	34	42	57	69	78	83	80	72	62	48	35	58
Av. Low °F	10	11	22	32	42	52	57	54	47	36	28	15	34
Humidity	V.Lo	V.Lo	V.Lo	V.Lo	Lo	Med	Med	Med	Med	V.Lo	V.Lo	V.Lo	V.Lo
Precip. Days	11	10	11	11	12	11	10	10	9	8	11	11	125
Precip. In.	2.7	2.4	2.8	2.9	3.0	3.3	3.1	2.9	3.1	2.7	4.0	3.3	36.2
Snowfall In.	17	16	11	2	<1	0	0	0	0	<1	4	14	64

HARTFORD, CONNECTICUT - 169 ft.

	JAN	FEB	MAR	APR	MAY	JUN	JUL	AUG	SEP	OCT	NOV	DEC	ANN.
Av. High °F	33	36	45	59	70	80	84	82	75	64	51	37	60
Av. Low °F	16	18	27	37	46	56	61	59	51	41	32	20	39
Humidity	V.Lo	V.Lo	V.Lo	V.Lo	Lo	Med	Hi	Hi	Med	Lo	V.Lo	V.Lo	Lo
Precip. Days	11	11	11	11	12	11	10	10	10	8	11	13	129
Precip. In.	3.3	3.2	3.9	3.7	3.5	3.5	3.4	4.0	3.5	3.0	4.3	4.1	43.4
Snowfall In.	11	13	12	2	0	0	0	0	0	0	2	13	53

NEW YORK CITY, NEW YORK - 314 ft.

	JAN	FEB	MAR	APR	MAY	JUN	JUL	AUG	SEP	OCT	NOV	DEC	ANN.
Av. High °F	39	40	48	61	71	81	85	83	77	67	54	41	62
Av. Low °F	26	27	34	44	53	63	68	66	60	51	41	30	47
Humidity	V.Lo	V.Lo	V.Lo	V.Lo	Lo	Med	Hi	Hi	Med	Lo	V.Lo	V.Lo	Lo
Precip. Days	11	10	12	11	11	10	11	10	8	8	9	10	121
Precip. In.	2.7	2.9	3.7	3.3	3.5	3.0	3.7	4.0	3.3	2.8	3.8	3.5	40.2
Snowfall In.	7	9	5	1	0	0	0	0	0	0	1	6	29

PHILADELPHIA, PENNSYLVANIA - 26 ft.

	JAN	FEB	MAR	APR	MAY	JUN	JUL	AUG	SEP	OCT	NOV	DEC	ANN.
Av. High °F	40	42	51	64	74	83	87	85	78	68	56	43	64
Av. Low °F	24	26	33	42	52	62	67	65	58	47	37	27	45
Humidity	V.Lo	V.Lo	V.Lo	V.Lo	Lo	Med	Hi	Hi	Med	Lo	V.Lo	V.Lo	Lo
Precip. Days	11	9	11	11	11	10	9	9	8	7	9	10	115
Precip. In.	2.8	2.6	3.7	3.3	3.4	3.7	4.1	4.1	3.0	2.5	3.4	3.3	39.9
Snowfall In.	5	6	4	<1	0	0	0	0	0	0	1	4	20

GREATEST U.S. PRECIPITATION IN ONE MINUTE: 1.2"
Unionville, Maryland - July 4, 1956

UNITED STATES
THE EAST

	JAN	FEB	MAR	APR	MAY	JUN	JUL	AUG	SEP	OCT	NOV	DEC	ANN.
PITTSBURGH, PENNSLYVANIA - 1,137 ft.													
Av. High °F	37	40	49	63	72	81	84	83	77	66	52	40	62
Av. Low °F	24	24	32	43	52	62	65	63	56	45	37	27	44
Humidity	V.Lo	V.Lo	V.Lo	V.Lo	Lo	Med	Hi	Hi	Med	Lo	V.Lo	V.Lo	Lo
Precip. Days	15	14	15	14	13	12	11	9	9	10	12	14	148
Precip. In.	2.6	2.3	3.6	3.4	3.6	3.7	3.8	3.2	2.5	2.5	2.5	2.5	36.2
Snowfall In.	7	7	6	1	0	0	0	0	0	<1	3	6	30
PORTLAND, MAINE - 43 ft.													
Av. High °F	31	33	41	53	64	73	79	78	70	60	48	35	55
Av. Low °F	12	13	23	33	42	51	57	55	47	38	30	16	35
Humidity	V.Lo	V.Lo	V.Lo	V.Lo	Lo	Med	Med	Med	Lo	V.Lo	V.Lo	V.Lo	V.Lo
Precip. Days	11	10	11	12	13	11	9	9	8	9	12	12	127
Precip. In.	3.4	3.5	3.6	3.5	3.3	3.1	2.6	2.6	3.1	3.3	4.9	4.1	40.8
Snowfall In.	18	20	14	3	<1	0	0	0	0	<1	3	16	74
PROVIDENCE, RHODE ISLAND - 51 ft.													
Av. High °F	36	38	45	57	67	76	81	80	73	64	52	40	59
Av. Low °F	21	21	29	38	47	57	63	61	54	43	35	23	41
Humidity	V.Lo	V.Lo	V.Lo	V.Lo	Lo	Med	Hi	Hi	Med	Lo	V.Lo	V.Lo	Lo
Precip. Days	11	11	12	11	11	11	9	10	9	8	11	12	126
Precip. In.	3.5	3.5	4.0	3.7	3.5	2.6	2.9	3.9	3.3	3.3	4.5	4.1	42.8
Snowfall In.	9	10	9	1	0	0	0	0	0	<1	<1	8	38
TRENTON, NEW JERSEY - 56 ft.													
Av. High °F	39	41	49	62	72	81	85	83	76	66	54	42	62
Av. Low °F	25	26	33	43	52	62	67	65	58	48	39	28	46
Humidity	V.Lo	V.Lo	V.Lo	V.Lo	Med	Med	Hi	Hi	Med	Lo	V.Lo	V.Lo	Lo
Precip. Days	11	10	12	11	12	10	10	10	8	8	10	11	123
Precip. In.	2.8	2.7	3.8	3.1	3.4	3.2	4.7	4.2	3.2	2.5	3.3	3.3	40.2
Snowfall In.	6	7	4	1	0	0	0	0	0	<1	<1	5	23
WASHINGTON, D.C. - 72 ft.													
Av. High °F	41	45	53	65	75	83	86	85	79	68	56	43	65
Av. Low °F	23	24	31	41	51	59	64	62	55	44	34	25	43
Humidity	V.Lo	V.Lo	V.Lo	Lo	Med	Hi	Hi	Hi	Med	Lo	V.Lo	V.Lo	Lo
Precip. Days	10	9	10	10	12	9	10	9	8	7	8	10	112
Precip. In.	2.8	2.6	3.5	3.0	3.7	3.6	4.1	4.2	3.3	2.7	3.1	3.5	40.1
Snowfall In.	5	7	3	<1	0	0	0	0	0	0	2	6	23

GREATEST U.S. SNOWFALL IN 24 HOURS: 76.0"
Silverlake, Colorado - April 14 to 15, 1921

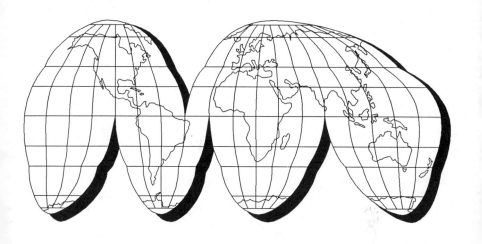

INTERNATIONAL

WEATHER

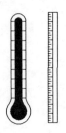

CONVERSIONS

LENGTH

1 inch (in.)	= 2.54 centimeters or 0.08 feet.
1 meter (m)	= 100 centimeters, 3.28 feet, or 39.37 inches.
1 centimeter (cm)	= 0.39 inch, 0.01 meter, or 10 millimeters.
1 kilometer (km)	= 1000 meters, 3,281 feet, or 0.62 mile.
1 mile (mi)	= 5280 feet, 1609 meters, or 1.61 kilometers.
1 degree latitude	= 111 kilometers or 60 nautical miles.

VOLUME & MASS

1 liter (l)	= 0.264 gallon (gal)
1 gram (g)	= 0.035 ounce, or 0.002 pound (lb)
1 kilogram (kg)	= 1000 grams or 2.2 pounds

SPEED

1 knot	= 1.15 mi/hr or 1.85 km/hr
1 mile per hour	= 0.87 knot or 1.61 km/hr
1 km per hour	= 0.54 knot or 0.62 mi/hr

PRESSURE

1 millibar (mb)	= 0.75 millimeter of mercury (mm Hg) or 0.02953 inch of mercury (in. Hg)
1 inch of mercury	= 33.865 millibars

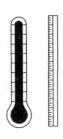

CONVERSIONS

TABLE: FAHRENHEIT TO CELCIUS

°F	0	1	2	3	4	5	6	7	8	9
110	43	44	44	45	46	46	47	47	48	48
100	38	38	39	39	40	41	41	42	42	43
90	32	33	33	34	34	35	36	36	37	37
80	27	27	28	28	29	29	30	31	31	32
70	21	22	22	23	23	24	24	25	26	26
60	16	16	17	17	18	18	19	19	20	21
50	10	11	11	12	12	13	13	14	14	15
40	4	5	6	6	7	7	8	8	9	9
30	-1	-1	0	1	1	2	2	3	3	4
20	-7	-6	-6	-5	-4	-4	-3	-3	-2	-2
10	-12	-12	-11	-11	-10	-9	-9	-8	-8	-7
0	-18	-17	-17	-16	-16	-15	-14	-14	-13	-13
-0	-18	-18	-19	-19	-20	-21	-21	-22	-22	-23
-10	-23	-24	-24	-25	-26	-26	-27	-27	-28	-28
-20	-29	-29	-30	-31	-31	-32	-32	-33	-33	-34
-30	-34	-35	-36	-36	-37	-37	-38	-38	-39	-39
-40	-40	-41	-41	-42	-42	-43	-43	-44	-44	-45
-50	-46	-46	-47	-47	-48	-48	-49	-49	-50	-51

TABLE: CELCIUS TO FAHRENHEIT

°C	0	1	2	3	4	5	6	7	8	9
40	104	106	108	109	111	113	115	117	118	120
30	86	88	90	91	93	95	97	99	100	102
20	68	70	72	73	75	77	79	81	82	84
10	50	52	54	55	57	59	61	63	64	66
0	32	34	36	37	39	41	43	45	46	48
-0	32	30	28	27	25	23	21	19	18	16
-10	14	12	10	9	7	5	3	1	-0	-2
-20	-4	-6	-8	-9	-11	-13	-15	-17	-18	-20
-30	-22	-24	-26	-27	-29	-31	-33	-35	-36	-38
-40	-40	-42	-44	-45	-47	-49	-51	-53	-54	-56
-50	-58	-60	-62	-63	-65	-67	-69	-71	-72	-74

 # GUIDELINES FOR WINTER TRAVEL

Weather conditions can change rapidly during the winter, especially in the mountains. To protect yourself from hazardous winter weather, follow these guidelines:

1. Plan your travel route carefully. Be aware of your primary and secondary travel routes.

2. Check the latest weather and road conditions.

3. Fill your gas tank before leaving.

4. If possible, do not travel alone.

5. If a storm becomes hazardous, seek refuge.

There are occasions when a storm will catch travelers off-guard. If you are caught in a blizzard, follow these instructions:

1. Stay inside your car and avoid exposure to the wind and cold.

2. Keep your window slightly open for ventilation and fresh air.

3. Run your motor and heater sparingly to prevent carbon monoxide poisoning. Avoid draining your car's battery.

4. Do not sleep or stay in one position. Exercise your hands and arms to keep good circulation.

5. Turn on your dome or parking lights to make your car visible, and keep watch.

CANADA

Some people claim it's the most beautiful country on Earth. It has a larger population of moose than people. The country stretches from the desolate polar wastelands in the north to the fertile plains of wheat in the south. Its western shores are drenched with generous rains. Majestic mountain peaks divide the country into two very different landscapes. In the eastern provinces the lush farmland looks more like Northern Europe than America.

Because of its northern latitude, all Canadian cities are cold in the winter - it's merely a matter of degree. British Columbia is the mildest province. Daytime highs in Vancouver average low 40's in the winter and upper 60's to mid-70's in the summer. Rain can be almost a daily occurrence there from October through April. The driest and warmest month is July, but even then rain can fall once or twice a week.

East of the Rockies the climate is much more extreme. Winnipeg's highs average near 80 in the summer, and below 10 in the winter. Fortunately, oppressive humidity is rare. The **best time to visit** the wheat belt is in *late summer.*

The major cities of eastern Canada are warmer than the plains in the winter, but still average below freezing. Summers are warm and humidity moderate. The least rainy month in Toronto is August with only nine wet days on average.

An **ideal time** to visit Canada - with warm temperatures, moderate humidity and low rainfall - would be *August.*

CANADA

	JAN	FEB	MAR	APR	MAY	JUN	JUL	AUG	SEP	OCT	NOV	DEC	ANN.
CALGARY (ALBERTA), CANADA - 3,540 ft.													
Av. High °F	24	28	37	53	63	69	76	74	64	54	38	29	51
Av. Low °F	2	6	14	27	36	43	47	45	37	29	17	9	26
Humidity	V.Lo	V.Lo	V.Lo	V.Lo	V.Lo	Lo	Lo	Lo	V.Lo	V.Lo	V.Lo	V.Lo	V.Lo
Precip. Days	7	8	10	8	11	12	10	10	8	7	5	5	101
Precip. In.	.5	.5	.8	1.0	2.3	3.1	2.5	2.3	1.5	.7	.7	.6	16.7
Snowfall In.	5	5	8	6	5	1	0	0	3	4	7	6	50
EDMONTON (ALBERTA), CANADA - 2,219 ft.													
Av. High °F	15	22	34	52	64	70	74	72	62	52	34	21	48
Av. Low °F	-4	1	12	28	38	45	49	47	38	30	16	5	25
Humidity	V.Lo	V.Lo	V.Lo	V.Lo	V.Lo	Lo	Med	Med	Lo	V.Lo	V.Lo	V.Lo	V.Lo
Precip. Days	12	9	10	8	12	15	14	12	9	9	11	12	133
Precip. In.	.9	.6	.8	.9	1.9	3.1	3.3	2.3	1.3	.7	.7	.8	17.3
Snowfall In.	9	7	7	5	2	0	0	0	1	4	8	8	51
MONTREAL (QUEBEC), CANADA - 187 ft.													
Av. High °F	21	23	33	50	64	74	78	75	67	54	39	26	50
Av. Low °F	6	8	19	33	47	57	61	59	51	40	27	13	35
Humidity	V.Lo	V.Lo	V.Lo	V.Lo	Lo	Med	Med	Med	Med	Lo	V.Lo	V.Lo	Lo
Precip. Days	15	14	14	12	12	13	12	11	12	13	14	15	157
Precip. In.	3.8	3.0	3.5	2.6	3.1	3.4	3.7	3.5	3.7	3.4	3.5	3.6	40.8
Snowfall In.	28	23	20	6	0	0	0	0	0	1	11	24	113
NIAGARA FALLS (ONTARIO), CANADA - 324 ft.													
Av. High °F	30	32	39	56	66	76	81	79	71	61	47	35	56
Av. Low °F	18	19	25	37	45	56	61	60	52	43	33	23	39
Humidity	V.Lo	V.Lo	V.Lo	V.Lo	Lo	Med	Hi	Med	Med	Lo	V.Lo	V.Lo	V.Lo
Precip. Days	18	17	16	12	12	11	10	9	11	13	15	19	163
Precip. In.	3.0	2.8	2.9	3.0	3.1	1.7	2.3	4.5	2.7	2.6	2.6	2.9	34.1
Snowfall In.	19	16	11	2	0	0	0	0	0	0	7	15	70
OTTAWA (ONTARIO), CANADA - 339 ft.													
Av. High °F	21	22	33	51	66	76	81	77	68	54	39	24	51
Av. Low °F	3	3	16	31	44	54	58	55	48	37	26	9	32
Humidity	V.Lo	V.Lo	V.Lo	V.Lo	Lo	Med	Med	Med	Lo	V.Lo	V.Lo	V.Lo	V.Lo
Precip. Days	13	12	12	11	11	10	11	10	11	12	12	14	139
Precip. In.	2.9	2.2	2.8	2.7	2.5	3.5	3.4	2.6	3.2	2.9	3.0	2.6	34.3
Snowfall In.	22	17	14	5	0	0	0	0	0	1	6	17	82.0

LOWEST U.S. & NORTH AMERICAN TEMPERATURE: -86°F
Near McGrath, Alaska (unofficial) - January 24, 1989

CANADA

	JAN	FEB	MAR	APR	MAY	JUN	JUL	AUG	SEP	OCT	NOV	DEC	ANN.
QUEBEC (QUEBEC), CANADA - 296 ft.													
Av. High °F	18	20	31	45	61	72	76	73	64	51	36	22	47
Av. Low °F	2	4	15	29	41	52	57	54	47	37	24	9	31
Humidity	V.Lo	V.Lo	V.Lo	V.Lo	Lo	Med	Med	Med	Med	V.Lo	V.Lo	V.Lo	V.Lo
Precip. Days	14	14	14	12	13	14	13	12	13	13	14	17	163
Precip. In.	3.5	2.7	3.0	2.3	3.1	3.7	4.0	4.0	3.6	3.4	3.2	3.2	39.7
Snowfall In.	29	23	21	9	1	0	0	0	0	2	14	25	124
TORONTO (ONTARIO), CANADA - 379 ft.													
Av. High °F	30	30	37	50	63	73	79	77	69	56	43	33	53
Av. Low °F	16	15	23	34	44	54	59	58	51	40	31	21	37
Humidity	V.Lo	V.Lo	V.Lo	V.Lo	Lo	Med	Med	Med	Med	Lo	V.Lo	V.Lo	V.Lo
Precip. Days	16	12	13	12	13	11	10	9	12	11	13	13	145
Precip. In.	2.7	2.4	2.6	2.5	2.9	2.7	2.9	2.7	2.9	2.4	2.8	2.6	32.1
Snowfall In.	16	15	11	3	0	0	0	0	0	1	4	12	62
VANCOUVER (BRITISH COLUMBIA), CANADA - 45 ft.													
Av. High °F	41	44	50	58	64	69	74	73	65	57	48	43	57
Av. Low °F	32	34	37	40	46	52	54	54	49	44	39	35	43
Humidity	V.Lo	V.Lo	V.Lo	Lo	Lo	Med	Med	Med	Med	Lo	Lo	V.Lo	Lo
Precip. Days	20	17	17	14	12	11	7	8	9	16	19	22	172
Precip. In.	8.6	5.8	5.0	3.3	2.8	2.5	1.2	1.7	3.6	5.8	8.3	8.8	57.4
Snowfall In.	12	6	3	0	0	0	0	0	0	0	2	6	29
VICTORIA (BRITISH COLUMBIA), CANADA - 228 ft.													
Av. High °F	43	46	50	56	61	65	68	68	64	57	49	45	56
Av. Low °F	36	36	39	42	46	50	53	53	50	46	42	38	44
Humidity	V.Lo	V.Lo	V.Lo	Lo	Lo	Med	Med	Med	Med	Lo	Lo	V.Lo	Lo
Precip. Days	19	15	15	11	9	8	4	5	9	14	19	19	147
Precip. In.	4.5	3.0	2.3	1.2	1.0	.9	.4	.6	1.5	2.8	4.3	4.7	27.2
Snowfall In.	6	5	1	0	0	0	0	0	0	0	1	1	14
WINNIPEG (MANITOBA), CANADA - 786 ft.													
Av. High °F	7	12	27	48	65	74	79	76	65	51	30	15	47
Av. Low °F	-13	-9	5	27	39	50	55	51	43	31	13	-3	24
Humidity	V.Lo	V.Lo	V.Lo	V.Lo	V.Lo	Med	Med	Med	Lo	V.Lo	V.Lo	V.Lo	V.Lo
Precip. Days	12	11	9	9	10	12	10	10	9	6	9	11	138
Precip. In.	.9	.9	1.2	1.4	2.3	3.1	3.1	2.5	2.3	1.5	1.1	.9	21.2
Snowfall In.	9	8	10	4	1	0	0	0	0	3	9	9	53

HIGHEST CANADIAN TEMPERATURE: 113°F
Midale, Saskatchewan - July 5, 1937

MEXICO

Mexico has a wide variety of climates that match its extreme geography. The country may be known for it's lush tropical beach resorts, but most of the land is mountainous, and includes some impressive volcanic peaks. The highest mountain can be found southeast of Mexico City. The volcano Popocatepetl soars to an impressive 17,883 feet above sea-level, and ten thousand feet higher than the city itself.

Mexico City has an unusual geographic setting. It lies in a high valley at an altitude of 7,575 feet and is surrounded by lofty, snow capped peaks. Thanks to it's altitude, temperatures in the city are mild despite its tropical latitude of 19 degrees north. The coolest month is January with a daytime average high of 66. The warmest month is May with highs in the upper 70's. Rainfall varies considerably, however, and by mid-summer it rains almost every day. Both July and August average 27 days of rain each. The best time to visit is in the early spring or late fall months when temperatures are warm and the rainfall infrequent. The **best months** are *March, April, and November.*

Mexico's tropical resorts are warm, or hot, and humid all year long. The rain comes in a distinct "season" and planning a trip around the rainfall is crucial. In Acapulco, Mazatlan or Puerto Vallarta very little rain falls from November through April. The driest months are March and April. The rainy "season" begins in May and reaches a peak in September when the days are steamy and heavy tropical downpours are the rule. In general, a trip to Mexico in the *spring* would find the **best overall** weather conditions.

MEXICO

	JAN	FEB	MAR	APR	MAY	JUN	JUL	AUG	SEP	OCT	NOV	DEC	ANN.
ACAPULCO, MEXICO - 10 ft.													
Av. High °F	87	87	87	87	89	89	90	91	89	89	89	88	89
Av. Low °F	72	72	72	73	76	77	76	77	76	76	74	73	75
Humidity	Hi	Hi	Hi	Hi	V.Hi	V.Hi	V.Hi	V.Hi	V.Hi	V.Hi	V.Hi	Hi	V.Hi
Precip. Days	0	0	0	0	2	12	15	14	17	10	1	1	72
Precip. In.	.3	0	0	0	1.5	10.9	11.1	8.7	15.1	6.2	1.3	.4	55.5
Snowfall In.	0	0	0	0	0	0	0	0	0	0	0	0	0
MAZATLAN, MEXICO - 256 ft.													
Av. High °F	71	71	73	76	80	84	86	86	85	85	80	75	79
Av. Low °F	61	62	63	65	70	76	77	77	77	76	71	65	70
Humidity	Med	Med	Hi	Hi	Hi	V.Hi	V.Hi	V.Hi	V.Hi	V.Hi	Hi	Hi	Hi
Precip. Days	.8	1	.3	0	.1	4	14	15	14	4	2	2	57
Precip. In.	.2	.3	0	0	0	1.2	6.6	10.6	11.9	1.2	.7	.7	33.4
Snowfall In.	0	0	0	0	0	0	0	0	0	0	0	0	0
MERIDA, MEXICO - 72 ft.													
Av. High °F	83	85	89	92	94	92	92	91	90	87	85	82	88
Av. Low °F	62	63	66	69	72	73	73	73	73	71	67	64	69
Humidity	Hi	Hi	Hi	Hi	Hi	V.Hi	V.Hi	V.Hi	V.Hi	V.Hi	Hi	Hi	Hi
Precip. Days	8	6	6	5	10	19	20	19	20	17	12	9	151
Precip. In.	1.0	.7	1.1	1.1	3.1	6.8	4.8	5.3	6.1	4.0	1.3	1.2	36.5
Snowfall In.	0	0	0	0	0	0	0	0	0	0	0	0	0
MEXICO CITY, MEXICO - 7,575 ft.													
Av. High °F	66	69	75	77	78	76	73	73	74	70	68	66	72
Av. Low °F	42	43	47	51	54	55	53	54	53	50	46	43	49
Humidity	V.Lo	V.Lo	V.Lo	Lo	Lo	Med	Med	Med	Med	Lo	Lo	V.Lo	Lo
Precip. Days	4	5	9	14	17	21	27	27	23	13	6	4	170
Precip. In.	.5	.2	.4	.8	2.1	4.7	6.7	6.0	5.1	2.0	.7	.3	29.4
Snowfall In.	0	0	0	0	0	0	0	0	0	0	0	0	0
PUERTO VALLARTA, MEXICO - 15 ft.													
Av. High °F	86	85	86	87	89	91	93	93	90	91	89	87	89
Av. Low °F	68	67	66	67	71	76	76	76	76	76	73	70	72
Humidity	Hi	Hi	Hi	Hi	Hi	V.Hi	V.Hi	V.Hi	V.Hi	V.Hi	V.Hi	Hi	V.Hi
Precip. Days	2	2	1	0	1	10	11	12	20	8	3	3	70
Precip. In.	.1	.2	0	0	.1	4.7	5.7	6.4	14.5	5.1	.9	1.8	39.5
Snowfall In.	0	0	0	0	0	0	0	0	0	0	0	0	0

LOWEST NORTH AMERICAN ANNUAL AVERAGE RAINFALL: 1.2"
Bataques, Mexico

60

SOUTH AMERICA

The most important thing to remember about the climate of South America is that its seasons are opposite those of the Northern Hemisphere - the warmest months occur during our winter, and the coolest temperatures happen during our summer. This presents a pleasant opportunity for those who like to get away from the cold and head for summer in January.

The primary South American travel destination has to be Rio. Its climate is sub-tropical with warm, humid conditions prevailing the year round. There is no distinct rainy "season" although the driest months are June through August. Even though this is their *winter*, daytime highs average mid-70's, and this may be the **best bet** for mild, dry conditions.

Buenos Aires is cooler than Rio, with temperatures that resemble California. Unlike the Golden State, however, rainfall is evenly spaced through the year and humidity is high from December through March. For a combination of moderate temperatures and humidity the **best times to visit** would be *October, November, and April.*

Caracas sits at an elevation of 3,418 feet and is much cooler than its latitude would imply (10° North). Temperatures are mild to warm all year, and humidity is moderate to high. Rainfall has a definite "season" and falls mostly from May through November. **Best months to visit** would be during the "dry" months of *January through March.* During *February* it rains on the average only two days, afternoon temperatures are in the upper 70's, and humidity is moderate - and that's hard to beat for an **ideal time to visit.**

SOUTH AMERICA & BERMUDA

	JAN	FEB	MAR	APR	MAY	JUN	JUL	AUG	SEP	OCT	NOV	DEC	ANN.

BUENOS AIRES (ARGENTINA), SOUTH AMERICA - 89 ft.

	JAN	FEB	MAR	APR	MAY	JUN	JUL	AUG	SEP	OCT	NOV	DEC	ANN.
Av. High °F	85	83	79	72	64	57	57	60	64	69	76	82	71
Av. Low °F	63	63	60	53	47	41	42	43	46	50	56	61	52
Humidity	Hi	Hi	Hi	Med	Med	Lo	Lo	Lo	Lo	Med	Med	Hi	Med
Precip. Days	7	6	7	8	7	7	8	9	8	9	9	8	93
Precip. In.	3.1	2.8	4.3	3.5	3.0	2.4	2.2	2.4	3.1	3.4	3.3	3.9	37.4

CARACAS (VENEZUELA), SOUTH AMERICA - 3,418 ft.

	JAN	FEB	MAR	APR	MAY	JUN	JUL	AUG	SEP	OCT	NOV	DEC	ANN.
Av. High °F	75	77	79	81	80	78	78	79	80	79	77	78	78
Av. Low °F	56	56	58	60	62	62	61	61	61	61	60	58	60
Humidity	Med	Med	Med	Hi	Hi	Hi	Hi	Hi	Hi	Hi	Hi	Med	Hi
Precip. Days	6	2	3	4	9	14	15	15	13	12	13	10	116
Precip. In.	.9	.4	.6	1.3	3.1	4.0	4.3	4.3	4.2	4.3	3.7	1.8	32.8

RIO DE JANEIRO (BRAZIL), SOUTH AMERICA - 201 ft.

	JAN	FEB	MAR	APR	MAY	JUN	JUL	AUG	SEP	OCT	NOV	DEC	ANN.
Av. High °F	84	85	83	80	77	76	75	76	75	77	79	82	79
Av. Low °F	73	73	72	69	66	64	63	64	65	66	68	71	68
Humidity	Hi	V.Hi	V.Hi	Hi	Hi	Hi	Hi	Hi	Hi	Hi	Hi	Hi	Hi
Precip. Days	13	11	12	10	10	7	7	7	11	13	13	14	128
Precip. In.	4.9	4.8	5.1	4.2	3.1	2.1	1.6	1.7	2.6	3.1	4.1	5.4	42.6

BERMUDA

Bermuda is a small island in the Atlantic about 875 miles east of Charleston, South Carolina. It has a pleasant climate - tropical in the summer, and mild in the winter. It rains quite a bit all year long. Summer humidity can be quite high. The **best months to visit** are *April through June.*

	JAN	FEB	MAR	APR	MAY	JUN	JUL	AUG	SEP	OCT	NOV	DEC	ANN.

HAMILTON, BERMUDA - 151 ft.

	JAN	FEB	MAR	APR	MAY	JUN	JUL	AUG	SEP	OCT	NOV	DEC	ANN.
Av. High °F	68	68	68	71	76	81	85	86	84	79	74	70	76
Av. Low °F	58	57	57	59	64	69	73	74	72	69	63	60	65
Humidity	Med	Med	Med	Med	Hi	Hi	V.Hi	V.Hi	V.Hi	Hi	Hi	Hi	Hi
Precip. Days	14	13	12	9	9	9	10	13	10	12	13	15	139
Precip. In.	4.4	4.7	4.8	4.1	4.6	4.4	4.5	5.4	5.2	5.8	5.0	4.7	57.6

BAHAMAS & CARIBBEAN

BAHAMAS

The climate of the Bahamas is tropical and much like South Florida. Temperatures are warm and the humidity high all year long. Rain falls primarily during June through October, peaking in September. The driest months are February and March. A late winter or early *spring* trip to Nassau would find the best weather conditions.

	JAN	FEB	MAR	APR	MAY	JUN	JUL	AUG	SEP	OCT	NOV	DEC	ANN.
NASSAU, BAHAMAS - 12 ft.
Av. High °F	77	77	79	81	84	87	88	89	88	85	81	79	83
Av. Low °F	65	64	66	69	71	74	75	76	75	73	70	67	70
Humidity	Hi	Hi	Hi	Hi	Hi	V.Hi	V.Hi	V.Hi	V.Hi	V.Hi	V.Hi	Hi	Hi
Precip. Days	6	5	5	6	9	12	14	14	15	13	9	6	114
Precip. In.	1.4	1.5	1.4	2.5	4.6	6.4	5.8	5.3	6.9	6.5	2.8	1.3	46.4

CARIBBEAN

Caribbean weather is tropical, warm, humid and rainy. It is also beautiful and dramatic. Humidity is always high. Rain is more plentiful during the summer, particularly August through October. The "Hurricane Season" runs from June through November, peaking in September. If you want to see the Caribbean at its best, *late winter or early spring* would be your best bet.

	JAN	FEB	MAR	APR	MAY	JUN	JUL	AUG	SEP	OCT	NOV	DEC	ANN.
BRIDGETOWN, BARBADOS - 181 ft.
Av. High °F	83	83	85	86	87	87	86	87	87	86	85	83	85
Av. Low °F	70	69	70	72	73	74	74	74	74	73	73	71	72
Humidity	Hi	Hi	Hi	Hi	Hi	Hi	V.Hi	V.Hi	V.Hi	V.Hi	V.Hi	Hi	Hi
Precip. Days	13	8	8	7	9	14	18	16	15	15	16	14	153
Precip. In.	2.6	1.1	1.3	1.4	2.3	4.4	5.8	5.8	6.7	7.0	8.1	3.8	50.2

CARIBBEAN & CEN. AMERICA

	JAN	FEB	MAR	APR	MAY	JUN	JUL	AUG	SEP	OCT	NOV	DEC	ANN.
KINGSTON, JAMAICA - 110 ft.													
Av. High °F	86	86	86	87	87	89	90	90	89	88	87	87	88
Av. Low °F	67	67	68	70	72	74	73	73	73	73	71	69	71
Humidity	Hi	Hi	Hi	Hi	V.Hi	V.Hi	V.Hi	V.Hi	V.Hi	V.Hi	V.Hi	Hi	V.Hi
Precip. Days	3	3	2	3	4	5	4	7	6	9	5	4	55
Precip. In.	.9	.6	.9	1.2	4.0	3.5	1.5	3.6	3.9	7.1	2.9	1.4	31.5
SAN JUAN, PUERTO RICO - 82 ft.													
Av. High °F	80	80	81	82	84	85	85	85	86	85	84	81	83
Av. Low °F	70	70	70	72	74	75	75	76	75	75	73	72	73
Humidity	Hi	Hi	Hi	V.Hi	V.Hi	V.Hi	V.Hi	V.Hi	V.Hi	V.Hi	V.Hi	V.Hi	V.Hi
Precip. Days	20	15	15	14	16	17	19	20	18	18	19	21	212
Precip. In.	4.3	2.7	2.9	4.1	5.9	5.4	5.7	6.3	6.2	5.6	6.3	5.4	60.8
ST. THOMAS, VIRGIN ISLANDS - 11 ft.													
Av. High °F	82	83	84	85	86	87	88	88	88	87	86	84	86
Av. Low °F	71	71	72	74	75	77	77	77	76	76	74	73	74
Humidity	Hi	Hi	Hi	Hi	V.Hi	V.Hi	V.Hi	V.Hi	V.Hi	V.Hi	V.Hi	V.Hi	V.Hi
Precip. Days	9	7	6	8	10	9	10	12	14	13	10	10	118
Precip. In.	2.5	1.9	1.7	2.2	4.6	3.2	3.3	4.1	6.9	5.6	3.9	3.9	43.8

CENTRAL AMERICA

Much of Central America is mountainous and covered with lush rain forests. The primary cities are in the interior, several thousand feet above sea level, where temperatures are mild all year long. The **driest months** are *December through March*. In San Jose, Costa Rica, and much of interior Central America, the driest month and least humid is *February*.

	JAN	FEB	MAR	APR	MAY	JUN	JUL	AUG	SEP	OCT	NOV	DEC	ANN.
SAN JOSE, COSTA RICA - 3,760 ft.													
Av. High °F	75	76	79	79	80	79	77	78	79	77	77	75	77
Av. Low °F	58	58	59	62	62	62	62	61	61	60	60	58	60
Humidity	Med	Med	Med	Hi	Hi	Hi	Hi	Hi	Hi	Hi	Hi	Hi	Hi
Precip. Days	3	1	2	7	19	22	23	24	24	25	14	6	170
Precip. In.	.6	.2	.8	1.8	9.0	9.5	8.3	9.5	12.0	11.8	5.7	1.6	70.8

EUROPE
SCANDINAVIA

Most of Scandinavia lies above of the 55 degree latitude line - placing it roughly as far north as Alaska. However, its climate is mild thanks to the warming influence of the Gulf Stream. This warm river of water flows north from the east coast of Florida then crosses the Atlantic and heads for the Norwegian and Irish coastlines. The Scandinavian climate would be much colder without its influence.

Generous rainfall bathes the mountainous west coast of Norway. These peaks squeeze so much water out of the clouds that roll in off the Atlantic that the fertile lands to the east are relatively dry and often sunnier than one might expect.

The **best time to visit** Scandinavia is in the *late spring and early summer.* The longest days occur in late June. Because of the latitude, summer nights are short and barely dark. Rainfall begins to increase in August, and from September through April the weather is uniformly chilly with frequent showers. Snow is common from November through March.

EUROPE
SCANDINAVIA

	JAN	FEB	MAR	APR	MAY	JUN	JUL	AUG	SEP	OCT	NOV	DEC	ANN.
BERGEN, NORWAY - 141 ft.													
Av. High °F	43	44	47	55	64	70	72	70	64	57	49	45	57
Av. Low °F	27	26	28	34	41	46	51	50	45	38	33	28	37
Humidity	V.Lo	V.Lo	V.Lo	V.Lo	Lo	Lo	Med	Med	Med	Lo	Lo	V.Lo	Lo
Precip. Days	18	14	13	13	11	13	13	16	17	18	16	18	180
Precip. In.	7.9	6.0	5.4	4.4	3.9	4.2	5.2	7.3	9.2	9.2	8.0	8.1	78.8
Snowfall In.	12	12	6	1	0	0	0	0	0	1	6	8	46
COPENHAGEN, DENMARK - 43 ft.													
Av. High °F	36	36	41	50	61	67	72	69	63	53	43	38	52
Av. Low °F	29	28	31	37	44	51	55	54	49	42	35	32	41
Humidity	V.Lo	V.Lo	V.Lo	V.Lo	Lo	Med	Med	Med	Med	Lo	V.Lo	V.Lo	Lo
Precip. Days	9	7	8	9	8	8	9	12	8	9	10	11	108
Precip. In.	1.6	1.3	1.2	1.7	1.7	2.1	2.2	3.2	1.9	2.1	2.2	2.1	23.3
Snowfall In.	6	5	3	1	0	0	0	0	0	1	4	5	25
HELSINKI, FINLAND - 30 ft.													
Av. High °F	27	26	32	43	55	63	71	66	57	45	37	31	46
Av. Low °F	17	15	22	31	41	49	57	55	46	37	30	22	35
Humidity	V.Lo	V.Lo	V.Lo	V.Lo	V.Lo	Lo	Med	Med	Lo	V.Lo	V.Lo	V.Lo	V.Lo
Precip. Days	11	8	8	8	8	9	8	12	11	12	11	11	117
Precip. In.	2.2	1.7	1.7	1.7	1.9	2.0	2.3	3.3	2.8	2.9	2.7	2.4	27.6
Snowfall In.	22	17	12	3	<1	0	0	0	0	6	10	19	89
OSLO, NORWAY - 308 ft.													
Av. High °F	30	32	40	50	62	69	73	69	60	49	37	31	50
Av. Low °F	20	20	25	34	43	51	56	53	45	37	29	24	36
Humidity	V.Lo	V.Lo	V.Lo	V.Lo	V.Lo	Lo	Med	Med	Lo	V.Lo	V.Lo	V.Lo	V.Lo
Precip. Days	8	7	7	7	7	8	10	11	8	10	9	10	102
Precip. In.	1.7	1.3	1.4	1.6	1.8	2.4	2.9	3.8	2.5	2.9	2.3	2.3	26.9
Snowfall In.	13	9	4	1	0	0	0	0	0	2	9	17	55
STOCKHOLM, SWEDEN - 146 ft.													
Av. High °F	31	31	37	45	57	65	70	66	58	48	38	33	48
Av. Low °F	23	22	26	32	41	49	55	53	46	39	31	26	37
Humidity	V.Lo	V.Lo	V.Lo	V.Lo	V.Lo	Lo	Med	Med	Lo	V.Lo	V.Lo	V.Lo	V.Lo
Precip. Days	8	7	7	6	8	7	9	10	8	9	9	9	97
Precip. In.	1.5	1.1	1.1	1.5	1.6	1.9	2.8	3.1	2.1	2.1	1.9	1.9	22.4
Snowfall In.	10	8	4	2	0	0	0	0	0	3	6	10	43

LOWEST GLOBAL TEMPERATURE: -127°F
Vostok, Antarctica - August 24, 1960

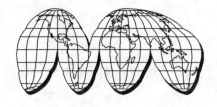

EUROPE
BRITISH ISLES

The warm Gulf Stream waters keep the British Isles warmer than their latitude would suggest. Most people correctly think of these islands as green, lush, cool, and damp. Rainfall in Ireland is spread uniformly through the year thus giving the Emerald Isle its classic color. June is the driest of the summer months.

England is also sunniest in June. Temperatures during the afternoon average near 70 until September. Rain falls on average two to three times a week all year so it's a good idea to expect it. Scotland has a similar rainfall pattern, but its a bit cooler than England. Again, the **best month** for sunshine and mild temperatures is *June*.

	JAN	FEB	MAR	APR	MAY	JUN	JUL	AUG	SEP	OCT	NOV	DEC	ANN.
BELFAST, NORTHERN IRELAND - 24 ft.													
Av. High °F	43	44	49	53	59	63	65	65	61	55	48	45	54
Av. Low °F	35	35	37	39	43	48	52	51	49	44	39	37	42
Humidity	V.Lo	V.Lo	V.Lo	Lo	Lo	Med	Med	Med	Med	Lo	Lo	Lo	Lo
Precip. Days	20	17	16	15	15	16	19	18	18	19	19	21	213
Precip. In.	4.1	2.8	2.4	2.4	2.5	2.4	3.4	3.5	3.3	3.9	3.6	3.9	38.2
Snowfall In.	7	6	4	1	0	0	0	0	0	0	1	4	23
DUBLIN, IRELAND - 155 ft.													
Av. High °F	47	47	51	54	59	65	67	67	63	57	51	47	56
Av. Low °F	35	35	36	38	42	48	51	51	47	43	38	36	42
Humidity	V.Lo	V.Lo	V.Lo	V.Lo	Lo	Lo	Med	Med	Med	Lo	Lo	Lo	Lo
Precip. Days	13	11	10	11	11	11	13	13	12	12	12	13	142
Precip. In.	2.7	2.2	2.0	1.9	2.3	2.0	2.8	3.0	2.8	2.7	2.7	2.6	29.7
Snowfall In.	2	3	1	0	0	0	0	0	0	0	1	1	6
GLASGOW, SCOTLAND - 29 ft.													
Av. High °F	43	44	48	53	59	64	66	65	61	54	47	43	54
Av. Low °F	34	35	36	38	42	47	52	51	47	43	37	36	41
Humidity	V.Lo	V.Lo	V.Lo	Lo	Lo	Med	Med	Med	Med	Lo	Lo	V.Lo	Lo
Precip. Days	21	17	15	15	15	15	17	18	17	19	19	20	208
Precip. In.	4.7	3.1	2.5	2.5	2.6	2.4	3.2	3.5	3.7	4.7	4.0	4.1	41.0
Snowfall In.	9	6	2	1	0	0	0	0	0	1	4	7	30

	JAN	FEB	MAR	APR	MAY	JUN	JUL	AUG	SEP	OCT	NOV	DEC	ANN.
LONDON, ENGLAND - 149 ft.													
Av. High °F	44	45	51	56	63	69	73	72	67	58	49	45	58
Av. Low °F	35	35	37	40	45	51	55	54	51	44	39	36	43
Humidity	V.Lo	V.Lo	V.Lo	V.Lo	Lo	Med	Med	Med	Med	Lo	Lo	V.Lo	Lo
Precip. Days	17	13	11	14	13	11	13	13	13	14	16	16	164
Precip. In.	2.0	1.5	1.4	1.8	1.8	1.6	2.0	2.2	1.8	2.3	2.5	2.0	22.9
Snowfall In.	2	1	0	0	0	0	0	0	0	0	0	1	4

CENTRAL EUROPE

Most of western France, the Low Countries, and northern Germany have a similar climate, especially during the prime travel months. Temperatures reach the 70's during summer afternoons, and nights are cool. Rain falls two or three times a week, but is less common in June and September. If you're looking for mild temperatures, long days, and the lowest chance of rainfall, *June* is the **month to visit** the continent. Months to be avoided would be November through March - unless you want to go skiing in the Alps.

The broad, low central European plain is broken by towering mountain ranges that create an entirely new climate of their own. Eastern and southern France, southern Germany, Austria, Switzerland, northern Italy and Czechoslovakia are hilly or mountainous - and so the climate here is as diverse as the geography.

The climate of Munich in southern Germany, gateway to the Alps, is wetter than the lowlands farther north. Here, it rains more in June and July than in any other months of the year. However, the region has such beauty that even an occasional wet day won't be too much of a disappointment.

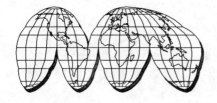

EUROPE
CENTRAL EUROPE

Geneva, Switzerland has a lull in the rain during July - **the best** of its summer months. Zurich is wetter than Geneva averaging 15 days of rainfall in July. Summer afternoons are warm with temperatures in the upper 70's. By September the rains ease off to one day in three and highs average near 70. Vienna is mild from May through September with rain falling every third day. August is the wettest summer month in this gorgeous Alpine city.

	JAN	FEB	MAR	APR	MAY	JUN	JUL	AUG	SEP	OCT	NOV	DEC	ANN.
AMSTERDAM, NETHERLANDS - 5 ft.													
Av. High °F	40	41	46	52	60	65	69	68	64	56	47	41	54
Av. Low °F	34	34	37	43	50	55	59	59	56	48	41	35	46
Humidity	V.Lo	V.Lo	V.Lo	Lo	Med	Med	Med	Med	Med	Lo	Lo	V.Lo	Lo
Precip. Days	19	15	13	14	12	12	14	14	15	18	19	19	184
Precip. In.	2.0	1.4	1.3	1.6	1.8	1.8	2.6	2.7	2.8	2.8	2.6	2.2	25.6
Snowfall In.	4	4	3	1	0	0	0	0	0	0	1	4	17
BERLIN, EAST GERMANY - 187 ft.													
Av. High °F	35	38	46	55	65	70	74	72	66	55	43	37	55
Av. Low °F	26	27	32	38	46	51	55	54	48	41	33	29	40
Humidity	V.Lo	V.Lo	V.Lo	V.Lo	Lo	Med	Med	Med	Lo	Lo	V.Lo	V.Lo	Lo
Precip. Days	10	8	9	9	8	9	10	10	8	8	8	11	108
Precip. In.	1.9	1.3	1.5	1.7	1.9	2.3	3.1	2.2	1.9	1.7	1.7	1.9	23.1
Snowfall In.	5	6	1	0	0	0	0	0	0	0	2	1	15
BRUSSELS, BELGIUM - 328 ft.													
Av. High °F	42	43	49	56	65	70	73	72	67	58	47	42	57
Av. Low °F	31	31	35	39	46	50	54	54	50	44	36	33	42
Humidity	V.Lo	V.Lo	V.Lo	Lo	Lo	Med	Med	Med	Med	Lo	V.Lo	V.Lo	Lo
Precip. Days	12	10	11	12	10	11	11	11	10	12	12	13	135
Precip. In.	2.6	2.0	2.4	2.5	2.5	2.6	3.5	3.0	2.6	3.0	3.1	3.2	33.0
Snowfall In.	4	3	1	0	0	0	0	0	0	0	2	5	15
FRANKFURT, WEST GERMANY - 338 ft.													
Av. High °F	37	42	49	58	67	72	75	74	67	56	45	39	57
Av. Low °F	29	31	35	41	48	53	56	55	51	43	36	31	42
Humidity	V.Lo	V.Lo	V.Lo	Lo	Lo	Med	Med	Med	Med	Lo	V.Lo	V.Lo	Lo
Precip. Days	9	9	9	9	9	9	10	10	9	9	9	11	112
Precip. In.	1.7	1.3	1.6	1.5	2.0	2.5	2.8	2.6	1.9	2.2	2.0	2.0	24.1
Snowfall In.	7	5	2	<1	0	0	0	0	0	<1	6	11	37

EUROPE
CENTRAL EUROPE

	JAN	FEB	MAR	APR	MAY	JUN	JUL	AUG	SEP	OCT	NOV	DEC	ANN.
GENEVA, SWITZERLAND - 1,329 ft.													
Av. High °F	39	43	51	58	66	73	77	76	69	58	47	40	58
Av. Low °F	29	30	35	41	48	55	58	57	52	44	37	31	43
Humidity	V.Lo	V.Lo	V.Lo	V.Lo	Lo	Med	Med	Med	Med	Lo	V.Lo	V.Lo	Lo
Precip. Days	10	9	10	11	12	11	9	10	10	11	11	10	124
Precip. In.	1.9	1.8	2.2	2.5	3.0	3.1	2.9	3.6	3.6	3.8	3.1	2.4	33.9
Snowfall In.	10	7	2	1	0	0	0	0	0	1	4	7	30
MUNICH, WEST GERMANY - 1,739 ft.													
Av. High °F	33	37	45	54	63	69	72	71	64	53	42	36	53
Av. Low °F	23	25	31	37	45	51	54	53	48	40	31	26	39
Humidity	V.Lo	V.Lo	V.Lo	V.Lo	Lo	Med	Med	Med	Med	Lo	V.Lo	V.Lo	Lo
Precip. Days	10	9	10	13	13	14	14	13	11	10	9	11	137
Precip. In.	1.7	1.4	1.9	2.7	3.7	4.6	4.7	4.2	3.2	2.2	1.9	1.9	34.1
Snowfall In.	12	11	3	2	1	0	0	0	0	2	3	10	44
PARIS, FRANCE - 164 ft.													
Av. High °F	42	45	52	60	67	73	76	75	69	59	49	43	59
Av. Low °F	32	33	36	41	47	52	55	55	50	44	38	33	43
Humidity	V.Lo	V.Lo	V.Lo	Lo	Lo	Med	Med	Med	Med	Lo	Lo	V.Lo	Lo
Precip. Days	15	13	15	14	13	11	12	12	11	14	15	17	162
Precip. In.	1.5	1.3	1.5	1.7	2.0	2.1	2.1	2.0	2.0	2.2	2.0	1.9	22.3
Snowfall In.	4	3	1	0	0	0	0	0	0	0	1	3	11
VIENNA, AUSTRIA - 664 ft.													
Av. High °F	34	38	47	57	66	71	75	73	66	55	44	37	55
Av. Low °F	26	28	34	41	50	56	59	58	52	44	36	30	43
Humidity	V.Lo	V.Lo	V.Lo	Lo	Lo	Med	Med	Med	Med	Lo	V.Lo	V.Lo	Lo
Precip. Days	8	7	7	9	9	9	9	10	7	8	8	9	100
Precip. In.	1.5	1.4	1.8	2.0	2.8	2.7	3.0	2.7	2.0	2.0	1.9	1.8	25.6
Snowfall In.	13	10	2	0	0	0	0	0	0	1	0	4	30
ZURICH, SWITZERLAND - 1,617 ft.													
Av. High °F	36	41	52	60	67	73	77	76	70	57	46	36	58
Av. Low °F	26	29	34	41	47	53	56	56	52	43	36	29	42
Humidity	V.Lo	V.Lo	V.Lo	V.Lo	Lo	Lo	Med	Med	Med	Lo	V.Lo	V.Lo	Lo
Precip. Days	10	8	9	12	13	15	14	13	11	11	10	10	136
Precip. In.	1.9	2.2	3.0	3.8	4.5	5.3	5.2	5.2	4.3	4.1	2.8	2.9	45.2
Snowfall In.	15	11	2	0	0	0	0	0	0	<1	18	26	72

LOWEST NORTHERN HEMISPHERIC TEMPERATURE: -90°F
Verkhoyansk, U.S.S.R. - February 7, 1892

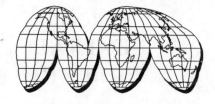

EUROPE
EASTERN
EUROPE

The **best time to visit** Eastern Europe is during the *late spring through early fall*. Temperatures are pleasantly warm during the days, the nights mild and the countryside kept green by occasional rainy days. Humidity is comfortable even during the summer. Winters can be quite cold as all of Eastern Europe falls under the grip of severe cold waves.

	JAN	FEB	MAR	APR	MAY	JUN	JUL	AUG	SEP	OCT	NOV	DEC	ANN.
BUDAPEST, HUNGARY - 394 ft.													
Av. High °F	35	40	51	62	72	78	82	81	74	61	47	38	60
Av. Low °F	26	28	36	44	52	57	61	59	53	45	37	31	44
Humidity	V.Lo	V.Lo	V.Lo	V.Lo	Lo	Med	Med	Med	Med	Lo	V.Lo	V.Lo	Lo
Precip. Days	7	6	7	8	9	8	7	6	7	8	8	9	90
Precip. In.	1.5	1.5	1.7	2.0	2.7	2.6	2.0	1.9	1.8	2.1	2.4	2.0	24.2
Snowfall In.	5	5	1	0	0	0	0	0	0	0	2	5	15
PRAGUE, CZECHOSLOVAKIA - 702 ft.													
Av. High °F	34	38	45	55	65	72	74	73	65	54	41	34	54
Av. Low °F	25	28	33	40	49	55	58	57	52	44	35	29	42
Humidity	V.Lo	V.Lo	V.Lo	V.Lo	Lo	Med	Med	Med	Lo	Lo	V.Lo	V.Lo	Lo
Precip. Days	12	11	13	12	13	14	14	12	11	11	12	13	148
Precip. In.	.9	.8	1.1	1.5	2.4	2.8	2.6	2.2	1.7	1.2	1.2	.9	19.3
Snowfall In.	7	6	3	1	0	0	0	0	0	2	7	7	32
SARAJEVO, YUGOSLAVIA - 2,067 ft.													
Av. High °F	37	42	51	62	69	75	80	81	75	60	50	41	60
Av. Low °F	24	27	33	40	47	53	56	56	51	42	36	29	41
Humidity	V.Lo	V.Lo	V.Lo	V.Lo	Lo	Med	Med	Med	Lo	Lo	V.Lo	V.Lo	Lo
Precip. Days	9	10	9	9	12	10	8	7	6	10	10	10	110
Precip. In.	2.5	2.8	2.1	1.9	3.4	3.3	2.4	2.3	2.6	3.6	3.7	3.5	34.1
Snowfall In.	25	23	13	5	1	0	0	0	0	3	17	22	109
WARSAW, POLAND - 394 ft.													
Av. High °F	30	32	41	54	67	72	75	73	65	54	40	32	53
Av. Low °F	21	23	28	38	48	53	56	55	48	41	32	25	39
Humidity	V.Lo	V.Lo	V.Lo	V.Lo	Lo	Med	Med	Med	Lo	Lo	V.Lo	V.Lo	V.Lo
Precip. Days	8	7	6	8	8	11	11	11	9	10	7	8	104
Precip. In.	1.2	1.1	1.3	1.5	1.9	2.6	3.0	3.0	1.9	1.7	1.4	1.4	22.0
Snowfall In.	11	9	4	1	0	0	0	0	0	1	5	9	40

LOWEST GLOBAL SEA LEVEL PRESSURE: 25.69"
520 miles northwest of Guam in the eye of Typhoon "Tip" - October 12, 1979

EUROPE
SPAIN & PORTUGAL

Lisbon's climate is almost identical to that of the coastal towns of Southern California. Summers are warm and dry, and winters are cool and wet. The **best months to visit** are *June through August* when temperatures are in the 70's during the day, 60's at night, and rain falls only once or twice a month. Spain is a bit drier - its mountains block the storms sweeping down from the north and west. Summers are very warm, and the humidity is tolerable. Daytime temperatures are in the 80's in most cities, nights average 50's or 60's, and rainfall is infrequent. The **best months to visit** are *May through September.* The driest month is August.

	JAN	FEB	MAR	APR	MAY	JUN	JUL	AUG	SEP	OCT	NOV	DEC	ANN.
BARCELONA, SPAIN - 312 ft.													
Av. High °F	56	57	61	64	71	77	81	82	78	71	62	57	68
Av. Low °F	42	44	47	51	57	63	69	69	65	58	50	44	55
Humidity	V.Lo	V.Lo	Lo	Lo	Med	Med	Hi	Hi	Med	Med	Lo	V.Lo	Lo
Precip. Days	5	7	7	8	8	5	4	5	7	8	7	6	77
Precip. In.	1.2	2.1	1.9	1.8	1.8	1.3	1.2	1.7	2.6	3.4	2.7	1.8	23.5
Snowfall In.	<1	0	0	0	0	0	0	0	0	0	0	<1	<1
LISBON, PORTUGAL - 313 ft.													
Av. High °F	56	58	61	64	69	75	79	80	76	69	62	57	67
Av. Low °F	46	47	49	52	56	60	63	64	62	57	52	47	55
Humidity	Lo	Lo	Lo	Lo	Med	Med	Med	Med	Med	Med	Lo	Lo	Lo
Precip. Days	9	8	10	7	6	2	1	6	4	7	10	10	75
Precip. In.	3.3	3.2	3.1	2.4	1.7	.7	.2	.2	1.4	3.1	4.2	3.6	27.0
Snowfall In.	0	0	0	0	0	0	0	0	0	0	0	0	0
MADRID, SPAIN - 2,188 ft.													
Av. High °F	47	51	57	64	71	80	87	86	77	66	54	48	66
Av. Low °F	33	35	40	44	50	57	62	62	56	48	40	35	47
Humidity	V.Lo	V.Lo	V.Lo	Lo	Lo	Med	Med	Med	Med	Lo	Lo	V.Lo	Lo
Precip. Days	9	9	11	9	9	6	3	2	6	8	10	9	91
Precip. In.	1.1	1.7	1.7	1.7	1.5	1.2	.4	.3	1.2	1.9	2.2	1.6	16.5
Snowfall In.	1	<1	0	0	0	0	0	0	0	0	0	<1	2

HIGHEST EUROPEAN TEMPERATURE: 122°F
Sevilla, Spain - August 4, 1881

EUROPE
THE RIVIERA,
ITALY & GREECE

THE RIVIERA

The Riviera enjoys warm, humid summers, and cool, showery winters. Because of the warm waters of the Mediterranean, the afternoon humidity can get rather "sticky" along this entire coastline. It can also rain in the summer - the driest month is July. Rainfall peaks in the winter, when temperatures are in the cool 50's during the day - much like California. **Best months to visit** are *May through October*. For the **ideal** combination of moderate temperature, humidity and rainfall, *June* would make an excellent choice.

	JAN	FEB	MAR	APR	MAY	JUN	JUL	AUG	SEP	OCT	NOV	DEC	ANN.
NICE, FRANCE - 39 ft.													
Av. High °F	56	56	59	64	69	76	81	81	77	70	62	58	67
Av. Low °F	40	41	45	49	56	62	66	66	62	55	48	43	53
Humidity	V.Lo	V.Lo	Lo	Lo	Med	Med	Hi	Hi	Hi	Med	Lo	V.Lo	Lo
Precip. Days	8	8	8	7	8	5	2	5	6	9	7	8	81
Precip. In.	2.4	2.4	3.2	1.9	2.8	1.0	.7	1.3	3.0	4.5	5.6	3.5	32.3
Snowfall In.	0	0	0	0	0	0	0	0	0	0	0	0	0

ITALY AND GREECE

While these two historical countries are thought of as generally sunny and warm, there are important differences in climate that can effect your travel plans. Italy gets more rain than Greece. It rains in Rome on the average of 76 days a year, and only 48 days in Athens. Rome has higher summer humidity. In the winter, their climates are almost the same.

The **best time to visit** Rome is in *June*. July and August are very warm and "muggy". By September and October the rain increases. If you are headed for Athens the **best months**

EUROPE
ITALY & GREECE

are *May, June,* September and October - particularly May. By October the rains return - but only one day a week on average. Mid-summer can be hot during the day with temperatures near 90 and humidity uncomfortable. Nights are warm with temperatures hovering in the 70's. Nights are cooler and more comfortable in May and October.

	JAN	FEB	MAR	APR	MAY	JUN	JUL	AUG	SEP	OCT	NOV	DEC	ANN.
ATHENS, GREECE - 351 ft.													
Av. High °F	54	55	60	67	77	85	90	90	83	74	64	57	71
Av. Low °F	42	43	46	52	60	67	72	72	66	60	52	46	57
Humidity	V.Lo	Lo	V.Lo	Lo	Med	Med	Med	Med	Med	Med	Med	Lo	Lo
Precip. Days	7	6	5	3	3	2	.7	.9	2	4	6	7	47
Precip. In.	2.2	1.6	1.4	.8	.8	.6	.2	.4	.6	1.7	2.8	2.8	15.8
Snowfall In.	1	<1	0	0	0	0	0	0	0	0	0	<1	2
NAPLES, ITALY - 220 ft.													
Av. High °F	54	55	60	67	73	81	86	86	81	72	63	57	70
Av. Low °F	40	41	45	49	56	62	66	66	62	55	48	43	53
Humidity	V.Lo	V.Lo	Lo	Lo	Med	Med	Hi	Hi	Hi	Med	Lo	V.Lo	Lo
Precip. Days	11	11	6	6	6	3	1	3	6	9	11	11	84
Precip. In.	4.8	3.5	1.7	1.8	2.2	.7	.6	1.3	4.3	4.6	4.1	4.7	34.3
Snowfall In.	1	0	0	0	0	0	0	0	0	0	0	0	1
ROME, ITALY - 377 ft.													
Av. High °F	54	56	62	68	74	82	88	88	83	73	63	56	71
Av. Low °F	39	39	42	46	55	60	64	64	61	53	46	41	51
Humidity	V.Lo	V.Lo	Lo	Lo	Med	Med	Hi	Hi	Med	Med	Lo	Lo	Med
Precip. Days	8	11	5	6	6	3	2	3	6	9	8	9	76
Precip. In.	2.7	2.3	1.5	1.7	2.0	1.0	.6	.9	2.7	3.7	3.8	2.8	25.7
Snowfall In.	1	<1	0	0	0	0	0	0	0	0	0	<1	2
VENICE, ITALY - 13 ft.													
Av. High °F	43	46	54	63	71	78	82	82	78	65	54	46	63
Av. Low °F	33	35	41	49	57	64	67	67	62	52	43	37	51
Humidity	V.Lo	V.Lo	V.Lo	Lo	Med	Hi	Hi	Hi	Hi	Med	Lo	V.Lo	Lo
Precip. Days	6	5	6	5	8	8	8	5	5	7	7	7	77
Precip. In.	1.6	1.8	2.0	1.6	3.2	2.6	2.8	1.7	2.4	3.4	3.1	2.4	28.6
Snowfall In.	2	2	<1	0	0	0	0	0	0	0	<1	1	6

GREATEST GLOBAL PRECIPITATION IN 1 YEAR: 1,041.78"
Cherrapunji, India - August 1860 to July 1861

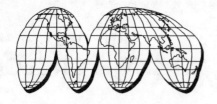

U.S.S.R.

The **best time to visit** the Soviet Union is the *summer.* It's simply too cold to really enjoy your trip at any other time of the year - unless you are visiting to see how people cope with the chilly temperatures!

Summer is the rainiest time of the year averaging one or two days of rain per week. Summer humidity in both Moscow and Leningrad is moderate. Daytime temperatures average in the 70's, and nights drop to the 50's. By October the highs average in the 40's and are regularly below freezing from November through March.

	JAN	FEB	MAR	APR	MAY	JUN	JUL	AUG	SEP	OCT	NOV	DEC	ANN.
LENINGRAD, U.S.S.R. - 16 ft.													
Av. High °F	23	24	33	45	58	66	71	66	57	45	34	26	46
Av. Low °F	12	12	18	31	42	51	57	53	45	37	27	18	33
Humidity	V.Lo	V.Lo	V.Lo	V.Lo	Lo	Lo	Med	Med	Lo	V.Lo	V.Lo	V.Lo	V.Lo
Precip. Days	17	15	13	11	12	12	13	15	14	15	17	18	173
Precip. In.	1.0	.9	.9	1.0	1.6	2.0	2.5	2.8	2.1	1.8	1.4	1.2	19.2
Snowfall In.	10	9	7	<1	0	0	0	0	0	4	9	12	51
MOSCOW, U.S.S.R. - 505 ft.													
Av. High °F	21	23	32	47	65	73	76	72	61	46	31	23	47
Av. Low °F	9	10	17	31	44	51	55	52	43	34	23	13	32
Humidity	V.Lo	V.Lo	V.Lo	V.Lo	Lo	Med	Med	Med	Lo	V.Lo	V.Lo	V.Lo	V.Lo
Precip. Days	11	9	8	9	9	10	12	12	9	11	10	9	119
Precip. In.	1.5	1.4	1.1	1.9	2.2	2.9	3.0	2.9	1.9	2.7	1.7	1.6	24.8
Snowfall In.	15	14	9	2	0	0	0	0	0	4	14	16	74

HIGHEST GLOBAL SEA LEVEL PRESSURE: 32.01"
Agata, Siberia U.S.S.R. - December 31, 1968

MIDDLE EAST
ISRAEL &
TURKEY

ISRAEL

The climate of Israel is marked by distinct seasons. Summers are warm, humid, and dry. Winters are cool, humidity is low, but rainfall plentiful. The spring months are the most pleasant. In particular the month of *April* offers the **best combination** of mild temperatures, moderate humidity, and few rainy days. Jerusalem has lower humidity than coastal areas because of its elevation - 2,485 feet. Towns bordering the Mediterranean can be quite humid during the summer.

	JAN	FEB	MAR	APR	MAY	JUN	JUL	AUG	SEP	OCT	NOV	DEC	ANN.
JERUSALEM, ISRAEL - 2,485 ft.													
Av. High °F	55	56	65	73	81	85	87	87	85	81	70	59	73
Av. Low °F	41	42	46	50	57	60	63	64	62	59	53	45	53
Humidity	V.Lo	V.Lo	V.Lo	V.Lo	Lo	Lo	Med	Med	Med	Lo	Lo	V.Lo	Lo
Precip. Days	9	11	3	3	1	0	0	0	0	1	4	7	39
Precip. In.	5.2	5.2	2.5	1.1	.1	0	0	0	0	.5	2.8	3.4	20.8
Snowfall In.	0	0	0	0	0	0	0	0	0	0	0	0	0
TEL AVIV, ISRAEL - 33 ft.													
Av. High °F	64	64	66	70	74	79	82	83	82	79	73	67	74
Av. Low °F	50	51	53	57	62	68	72	74	71	65	58	53	61
Humidity	Lo	Lo	Med	Med	Hi	Hi	V.Hi	V.Hi	Hi	Hi	Med	Lo	Med
Precip. Days	9	5	5	2	2	0	0	2	1	1	6	12	45
Precip. In.	4.6	2.4	2.0	1.0	1.4	0	0	1.7	.2	.5	4.8	12.9	31.5
Snowfall In.	0	0	0	0	0	0	0	0	0	0	0	0	0

TURKEY

The primary business and tourist center of Turkey is the historic city of Istanbul. Summers are warm and humid with occasional rainfall. Winters are chilly with frequent rainy days. The **best times to visit** are *late spring or early fall*. In particular, *May* offers the best mix of the elements, although it does rain on five days during that month.

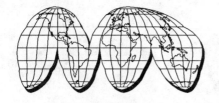

MIDDLE EAST
SAUDI ARABIAN PENINSULA

	JAN	FEB	MAR	APR	MAY	JUN	JUL	AUG	SEP	OCT	NOV	DEC	ANN.
ISTANBUL, TURKEY - 59 ft.													
Av. High °F	45	47	52	61	68	77	81	81	75	67	59	51	64
Av. Low °F	36	37	39	45	53	60	65	66	61	54	48	41	50
Humidity	V.Lo	V.Lo	Lo	Lo	Med	Hi	Hi	Hi	Hi	Med	Lo	Lo	Med
Precip. Days	12	10	9	6	5	4	3	3	5	9	11	15	92
Precip. In.	3.7	2.3	2.6	1.9	1.4	1.3	1.7	1.5	2.3	3.8	4.1	4.9	31.5
Snowfall In.	8	6	0	0	0	0	0	0	0	0	0	2	16

SAUDI ARABIAN PENINSULA

The oil producing lands of the peninsula are know for their hot and dry summers with afternoon temperatures averaging above 100 degrees. However, winter temperatures are pleasant. The **best months to visit** are late *fall and early spring. November and March* offer a nice combination of mild temperatures, low humidity and sunny skies with few rainy days. Months to avoid are May through October, and in particular July and August - unless you like it hot with nights staying in the 70's and 80's!

	JAN	FEB	MAR	APR	MAY	JUN	JUL	AUG	SEP	OCT	NOV	DEC	ANN.
KUWAIT CITY, KUWAIT - 16 ft.													
Av. High °F	61	65	72	83	94	98	103	104	100	91	77	65	85
Av. Low °F	49	51	59	68	77	82	86	86	81	73	62	53	69
Humidity	Lo	Lo	Lo	Med	Med	Lo	Med	Med	Med	Med	Med	Lo	Lo
Precip. Days	3	3	3	1	0	0	0	0	0	1	2	3	16
Precip. In.	.9	.9	1.1	.2	0	0	0	0	0	.1	.6	1.1	5.1
Snowfall In.	0	0	0	0	0	0	0	0	0	0	0	0	0
RIYADH, SAUDIA ARABIA - 1,938 ft.													
Av. High °F	70	73	82	89	100	107	107	107	102	94	84	70	90
Av. Low °F	46	48	56	64	72	77	78	75	72	61	55	49	63
Humidity	V.Lo	V.Lo	V.Lo	Lo	Lo	V.Lo	V.Lo	V.Lo	V.Lo	V.Lo	Lo	V.Lo	V.Lo
Precip. Days	1	1	3	4	1	0	0	0	0	0	0	0	10
Precip. In.	.1	.8	.9	1.0	.4	0	0	0	0	0	0	0	3.2
Snowfall In.	0	0	0	0	0	0	0	0	0	0	0	0	0

INDIA

Many people think of India as always hot and humid. However, some months can be very pleasant with *winter* the **best time to visit.** *February* is generally ideal all around for moderate temperature, humidity, and low rainfall. Summers are to be avoided. Not only are they hot, but the humidity is high and rainfall heavy. In February it rains only once on average and the highs reach 83 with moderate humidity.

New Delhi's climate can be extreme. In May, just before the Monsoon rains arrive, highs average 105 - in January highs average 70 with chilly nights dropping to 44. The general rule is that the farther north you travel the cooler it gets, although most of the country lies either in the tropics or sub-tropics and is surrounded by the warm waters of the Bay of Bengal and the Arabian Sea.

	JAN	FEB	MAR	APR	MAY	JUN	JUL	AUG	SEP	OCT	NOV	DEC	ANN.
BOMBAY, INDIA - 37 ft.													
Av. High °F	83	83	86	89	91	89	85	85	85	89	89	87	87
Av. Low °F	67	67	72	76	80	79	77	76	76	76	73	69	74
Humidity	Med	Med	Hi	V.Hi	V.Hi	V.Hi	V.Hi	V.Hi	V.Hi	V.Hi	Hi	Med	Hi
Precip. Days	1	1	1	0	2	18	23	21	15	5	3	1	91
Precip. In.	.1	.1	.1	0	.7	19.1	24.3	13.4	10.4	2.5	.5	.1	71.2
CALCUTTA, INDIA - 21 ft.													
Av. High °F	80	84	93	97	96	92	89	89	90	89	84	79	89
Av. Low °F	55	59	69	75	77	79	79	78	78	74	64	55	70
Humidity	Med	Med	Hi	V.Hi	V.Hi	V.Hi	V.Hi	V.Hi	V.Hi	V.Hi	Hi	Med	Hi
Precip. Days	3	5	5	6	10	16	18	18	13	6	3	2	105
Precip. In.	.4	1.2	1.4	1.7	5.5	11.7	12.8	12.9	9.9	4.5	.8	.2	63.0
NEW DELHI, INDIA - 714 ft.													
Av. High °F	70	75	87	97	105	102	96	93	93	93	84	73	89
Av. Low °F	44	49	58	68	79	83	81	79	75	65	52	46	65
Humidity	Lo	Lo	Lo	Med	Med	Hi	V.Hi	V.Hi	V.Hi	Hi	Lo	Lo	Med
Precip. Days	2	2	1	1	2	4	8	8	4	1	.2	1	34
Precip. In.	.9	.7	.5	.3	.5	2.9	7.1	6.8	4.6	.4	.1	.4	25.2

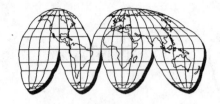

AFRICA

The continent of Africa contains a wide variety of climates, ranging from extremely wet and tropical to extremely dry and barren. Along the coast of South Africa the climate can be as pleasant as any in the world. In the African interior the climate can be as hostile as any on the planet.

Along the Mediterranean temperatures are mild and the rainfall infrequent. Casablanca boasts a superb climate marred only by high humidity in the summer. The **best months to visit** are *May and October.*

It's **best to visit Egypt** and the pyramids in the *spring or fall - especially April and November.* Summers are hot, humid, and dry. Even in the winter rainfall is scant, but temperatures modify and resemble Los Angeles in January. All months except June through September are tolerably mild.

A visit to Kenya and Mount Kilimanjaro will take you to the city of Nairobi at 5,971 ft. elevation. Temperatures here are uniformly comfortable all year long with highs ranging from 69 to 79 during the afternoon and night in the 50's. Rainfall increases during March through May, with heavy amounts expected several times a week.

The best time to visit is during the dry months of *June through September - particularly September.*

AFRICA

South Africa is a land of mountains and beaches - spectacular scenery and a climate to match. Johannesburg can get quite cool in the Southern Hemisphere winter season of May through September. Temperatures are mild during the summer, but rains are common at that time.

The best months to visit are in the *spring and fall* if you want daytime temperatures in the 70's and rainfall that isn't too frequent.

At lower elevations the weather can seem much like the Southern California beach cities with mild temperatures, low rainfall, and miles of beaches and surf for scenery. Any month from *November through March* would be enjoyable.

AFRICA

	JAN	FEB	MAR	APR	MAY	JUN	JUL	AUG	SEP	OCT	NOV	DEC	ANN.
CAIRO (EGYPT), AFRICA - 381 ft.													
Av. High °F	65	69	75	83	91	95	96	95	90	86	78	68	83
Av. Low °F	47	48	52	57	63	68	70	71	68	65	58	50	60
Humidity	Lo	V.Lo	Lo	Lo	Med	Med	Hi	Hi	Hi	Med	Med	Lo	Med
Precip. Days	1	1	1	<1	<1	0	0	0	0	<1	1	1	5
Precip. In.	.2	.2	.2	.1	.1	0	0	0	0	0	.1	.2	1.1
Snowfall In.	0	0	0	0	0	0	0	0	0	0	0	0	0
CAPETOWN (SOUTH AFRICA), AFRICA - 56 ft.													
Av. High °F	69	70	69	66	64	62	60	61	63	65	67	69	65
Av. Low °F	56	56	56	54	53	51	50	50	50	53	54	55	53
Humidity	Med	Med	Med	Med	Med	Med	Lo	Med	Lo	Med	Med	Med	Med
Precip. Days	3	2	3	6	9	9	10	9	7	5	3	3	69
Precip. In.	.1	.1	.3	.9	1.3	1.7	1.6	1.0	1.0	.5	.2	.3	9.0
Snowfall In.	0	0	0	0	0	0	0	0	0	0	0	0	0
CASABLANCA (MOROCCO), AFRICA - 164 ft.													
Av. High °F	63	64	67	69	72	76	79	81	79	76	69	65	72
Av. Low °F	45	46	49	52	56	61	65	66	63	58	52	47	55
Humidity	Lo	Lo	Med	Med	Med	Hi	Hi	Hi	Hi	Med	Med	Med	Med
Precip. Days	8	8	8	7	5	1	0	0	1	6	8	9	61
Precip. In.	2.1	1.9	2.2	1.4	.9	.2	0	0	.3	1.5	2.6	2.8	15.9
Snowfall In.	0	0	0	0	0	0	0	0	0	0	0	0	0
JOHANNESBURG (SOUTH AFRICA), AFRICA - 5,463 ft.													
Av. High °F	78	77	75	72	66	62	63	68	73	77	77	78	72
Av. Low °F	58	58	55	50	43	39	39	43	48	53	55	57	50
Humidity	Med	Med	Med	Med	Lo	Lo	Lo	Lo	Lo	Med	Med	Med	Med
Precip. Days	12	9	9	4	3	1	.9	.9	2	7	10	11	70
Precip. In.	4.5	4.3	3.5	1.5	1.0	.3	.3	.3	.9	2.2	4.2	4.9	27.9
Snowfall In.	0	0	0	0	0	0	0	0	0	0	0	0	0
NAIROBI (KENYA), AFRICA - 5,971 ft.													
Av. High °F	77	79	77	75	72	70	69	70	75	76	74	74	74
Av. Low °F	54	55	57	58	56	53	51	52	52	55	56	55	55
Humidity	Med	Med	Med	Hi	Med	Med	Med	Med	Med	Med	Med	Med	Med
Precip. Days	5	6	11	16	17	9	6	7	6	8	15	11	117
Precip. In.	1.5	2.5	4.9	8.3	6.2	1.8	.6	.9	1.2	2.1	4.3	3.4	37.7
Snowfall In.	0	0	0	0	0	0	0	0	0	0	0	0	0

HIGHEST GLOBAL TEMPERATURE: 136°F
El Azizia, Libya - September 13, 1922

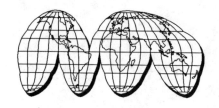

CHINA

China is uniformly warm, humid, and rainy in the summer. In contrast, winter weather can vary considerably from city to city. Beijing, for example, is very cold in the winter with afternoon highs averaging only 34 degrees. Shanghai's January high is only 46. Hong Kong's tropical climate keeps it mild even in January - highs are in the 60's. Rainfall in China is concentrated primarily in the summer months - July in particular is to be avoided due to its high heat, humidity, and generous rainfall.

The **best times to visit** Beijing are in the *early fall and late spring - especially May and September,* with *April and October* almost as pleasant. Humidity, however, can be high from June through September. Shanghai is very pleasant in October and May. Taiwan is driest in the winter. Humidity there is high from April through October. Hong Kong's **best months** are *November through April.* Humidity there is very high from May through September. Rainfall can be torrential in June through August and the island is visited by occasional typhoons (hurricanes) at that time.

	JAN	FEB	MAR	APR	MAY	JUN	JUL	AUG	SEP	OCT	NOV	DEC	ANN.
BEIJING, CHINA - 167 ft.													
Av. High °F	34	43	54	69	81	88	89	86	79	66	50	39	65
Av. Low °F	15	21	32	44	56	65	72	69	58	44	31	20	44
Humidity	V.Lo	V.Lo	Lo	Med	Med	Hi	V.Hi	V.Hi	Hi	Med	Lo	V.Lo	Med
Precip. Days	2	2	2	3	5	8	15	11	8	2	1	2	61
Precip. In.	.2	.2	.3	.6	1.3	3.3	9.8	5.7	2.3	.7	.2	.1	24.7
Snowfall In.	7	4	1	0	0	0	0	0	0	0	1	3	16

HIGHEST ASIAN TEMPERATURE: 129°F
Tirat Tsvi, Israel - June 21, 1942

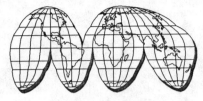

ASIA
CHINA & JAPAN

	JAN	FEB	MAR	APR	MAY	JUN	JUL	AUG	SEP	OCT	NOV	DEC	ANN.
HONG KONG, CHINA - 109 ft.													
Av. High °F	64	63	67	75	82	85	87	87	85	81	74	68	77
Av. Low °F	56	55	60	67	74	78	78	78	77	73	65	59	68
Humidity	Med	Med	Med	Hi	V.Hi	V.Hi	V.Hi	V.Hi	V.Hi	Hi	Hi	Med	Hi
Precip. Days	4	5	7	8	13	18	17	15	12	6	2	3	110
Precip. In.	1.3	1.8	2.9	5.4	11.5	15.5	15.0	14.2	10.1	4.5	1.7	1.2	85.1
Snowfall In.	0	0	0	0	0	0	0	0	0	0	0	0	0
SHANGHAI, CHINA - 23 ft.													
Av. High °F	46	47	55	66	77	82	90	90	82	74	63	53	69
Av. Low °F	33	34	40	50	59	67	74	74	66	57	45	36	53
Humidity	V.Lo	V.Lo	Lo	Med	Med	Hi	V.Hi	V.Hi	Hi	Med	Lo	V.Lo	Med
Precip. Days	6	9	9	9	9	11	9	9	11	4	6	6	98
Precip. In.	1.9	2.3	3.3	3.7	3.7	7.1	5.8	5.6	5.1	2.8	2.0	1.4	44.7
Snowfall In.	0	0	0	0	0	0	0	0	0	0	0	0	0
TAIPEI, CHINA - 30 ft.													
Av. High °F	66	65	70	77	83	89	92	91	88	81	75	69	79
Av. Low °F	54	53	57	63	69	73	76	75	73	67	62	57	65
Humidity	Med	Med	Med	Hi	V.Hi	V.Hi	V.Hi	V.Hi	V.Hi	Hi	Hi	Med	Hi
Precip. Days	9	13	12	14	12	13	10	12	10	9	7	8	129
Precip. In.	3.4	5.3	7.0	6.7	9.1	11.4	9.1	12.0	9.6	4.8	2.6	2.8	83.8
Snowfall In.	0	0	0	0	0	0	0	0	0	0	0	0	0

JAPAN

Japan is also very warm, humid, and wet in the summer. Winters can be chilly. The best month to visit Tokyo is May. Rainfall there peaks in September and October. Osaka is a bit warmer than Tokyo and can also be extremely humid and wet during the summer. *May and October* are the **best months to visit.**

ASIA
JAPAN &
SOUTH KOREA

	JAN	FEB	MAR	APR	MAY	JUN	JUL	AUG	SEP	OCT	NOV	DEC	ANN.
OSAKA, JAPAN - 10 ft.													
Av. High °F	47	48	54	65	73	80	87	90	83	72	62	52	68
Av. Low °F	32	33	37	47	55	64	73	74	67	55	44	37	51
Humidity	V.Lo	V.Lo	V.Lo	Lo	Med	Hi	V.Hi	V.Hi	Hi	Med	Lo	V.Lo	Med
Precip. Days	6	6	9	10	10	11	9	7	11	9	7	6	101
Precip. In.	1.7	2.3	3.8	5.2	4.9	7.4	5.9	4.4	7.0	5.1	3.0	1.9	52.6
Snowfall In.	1	1	0	0	0	0	0	0	0	0	0	0	2
TOKYO, JAPAN - 19 ft.													
Av. High °F	47	48	54	63	71	76	83	86	79	69	60	52	66
Av. Low °F	29	31	36	46	54	63	70	72	66	55	43	33	50
Humidity	V.Lo	V.Lo	V.Lo	Lo	Med	Hi	V.Hi	V.Hi	Hi	Med	Lo	V.Lo	Med
Precip. Days	5	6	10	10	10	12	10	9	12	11	7	5	107
Precip. In.	1.9	2.9	4.2	5.3	5.8	6.5	5.6	6.0	9.2	8.2	3.8	2.2	61.6
Snowfall In.	2	5	1	0	0	0	0	0	0	0	0	0	8

SOUTH KOREA

South Korea's climate can be extreme - very cold in the winter and tropical in the summer. Rain is most common in July and August. The **most enjoyable months to visit** are *May and late September through early October.*

	JAN	FEB	MAR	APR	MAY	JUN	JUL	AUG	SEP	OCT	NOV	DEC	ANN.
SEOUL, SOUTH KOREA - 285 ft.													
Av. High °F	32	37	47	62	72	80	84	87	78	67	51	37	61
Av. Low °F	15	20	29	41	51	61	70	71	59	45	32	20	43
Humidity	V.Lo	V.Lo	V.Lo	Lo	Med	Hi	V.Hi	V.Hi	Hi	Lo	V.Lo	V.Lo	Lo
Precip. Days	8	6	7	8	10	10	16	13	9	7	9	9	112
Precip. In.	1.2	.8	1.5	3.0	3.2	5.1	14.8	10.5	4.7	1.6	1.8	1.0	49.2
Snowfall In.	5	4	1	0	0	0	0	0	0	0	0	1	11

GREATEST GLOBAL PRECIPITATION IN 1 MONTH: 366.14"
Cherrapunji, India - July 1861

ASIA
PHILIPPINES &
S.E. ASIA

The Philippines, and all of Southeast Asia, are tropical, and hence uniformly warm, humid, and rainy. However, there is a dry season in Manila and Bangkok, while Singapore is rainy all year long. The **best time to visit** Manila is in *January and February* when rainfall is light and temperatures are moderately warm.

Months to be avoided are June through September. Bangkok and much of Southeast Asia have a dry season during the winter months. **Best months to visit** are *December through February*. Bangkok is wettest in September, although May through August are also very rainy.

	JAN	FEB	MAR	APR	MAY	JUN	JUL	AUG	SEP	OCT	NOV	DEC	ANN.
BANGKOK, THAILAND - 7 ft.													
Av. High °F	89	91	93	95	93	91	90	90	89	88	87	87	90
Av. Low °F	68	72	75	77	77	76	76	76	76	75	72	68	74
Humidity	Hi	V.Hi	V.Hi	V.Hi	V.Hi	V.Hi	V.Hi	V.Hi	V.Hi	V.Hi	V.Hi	Hi	V.Hi
Precip. Days	1	1	3	3	9	10	13	13	15	14	5	1	88
Precip. In.	.3	.8	1.4	2.3	7.8	6.3	6.3	6.9	12.0	8.1	2.6	.2	55.0
MANILA, PHILIPPINES - 47 ft.													
Av. High °F	86	88	91	93	93	91	88	87	88	88	87	86	89
Av. Low °F	69	69	71	73	75	75	75	75	75	74	72	70	73
Humidity	Hi	Hi	Hi	V.Hi	V.Hi	V.Hi	V.Hi	V.Hi	V.Hi	V.Hi	V.Hi	V.Hi	V.Hi
Precip. Days	6	3	4	4	12	17	24	23	22	19	14	11	159
Precip. In.	.9	.5	.7	1.3	5.1	10.0	17.0	16.6	14.0	7.6	5.7	2.6	82.0
SINGAPORE, SINGAPORE - 33 ft.													
Av. High °F	86	88	88	88	89	88	88	87	87	87	87	87	87
Av. Low °F	73	73	75	75	75	75	75	75	75	74	74	74	74
Humidity	V.Hi	V.Hi	V.Hi	V.Hi	V.Hi	V.Hi	V.Hi	V.Hi	V.Hi	V.Hi	V.Hi	V.Hi	V.Hi
Precip. Days	17	11	14	15	15	13	13	14	14	16	18	19	179
Precip. In.	9.9	6.8	7.6	7.4	6.8	6.8	6.7	7.7	7.0	8.2	10.0	10.1	95.0

LOWEST GLOBAL AVERAGE ANNUAL RAINFALL: 0.03"
Arica, Chile

BEAUFORT WIND SCALE

Beaufort Number	Explanatory Titles	Land Specifications	Miles Per Hour	Forecast Terms
0	Calm	Smoke rises vertically.	Less Than 1	Light
1	Light air	Direction of wind shown by smoke drift, but not by wind vanes.	1-3	Light
2	Slight Breeze	Wind felt on face; leaves rustle; ordinary vane moved by wind.	4-7	Light
3	Gentle Breeze	Leaves and small twigs in constant motion; small branches moved.	8-12	Gentle
4	Mod. Breeze	Raises dust and loose paper; small branches are moved.	13-18	Moderate
5	Fresh Breeze	Small trees in leaf begin to sway; crested wavelets form on inland water.	19-24	Fresh
6	Strong Breeze	Large branches in motion; whistling umbrellas used with difficulty.	25-31	Strong
7	High Wind	Whole trees in motion; inconvenience felt in walking against wind.	32-38	Strong
8	Gale	Breaks twigs off trees; generally impedes progress.	39-46	Gale
9	Strong Gale	Slight structural damage occurs (chimney pots and slate removed)	47-54	Gale
10	Whole Gale	Seldom experienced inland; trees uprooted; considerable damage.	55-63	Whole Gale
11	Storm	Very rarely experienced; accompanied by widespread damage.	64-75	Whole Gale
12	Hurricane	Extensive damage.	Above 75	Hurricane

AUSTRALIA

Three primary climates dominate the continent of Australia. The north is tropical warm, humid and rainy. Most of the interior is hot, barren, and rather desolate. The coastal strip is generally warm and somewhat humid. Rainfall varies from generous in Queensland to sparse in Victoria. This narrow, flat, scenic plain is home to most Australians and boasts some of the most beautiful and pleasant weather.

For year round mild to warm temperatures few areas can top coastal Queensland near Brisbane. In general the weather is a match for Hawaii or other semi-tropical resort areas. The **best months to visit** are *May, and September through October* - before the humidity and rainfall increase.

The greater Sydney area boasts a magnificent, mild temperature pattern. Rainfall, cloudiness, and humidity can be a problem at times. The **best combination** of moderate temperature and humidity with the least rainfall would be found during *October through December.*

The climate of Melbourne is much like that of coastal California. It does get chilly here during the Southern Hemisphere winter months of June through August. **Best months to visit** are in the *November through March, especially February.*

If you want to visit the interior, you'll find Alice Springs a good base. It's hot in the summer, cool in the winter, and averages less than 10 inches of rain per year.

Perth, in Western Australia boasts a warm climate with moderate rainfall. The driest months are August and September.

AUSTRALIA

	JAN	FEB	MAR	APR	MAY	JUN	JUL	AUG	SEP	OCT	NOV	DEC	ANN.

ALICE SPRINGS (NORTHERN TERRITORY), AUSTRALIA - 1,901 ft.

	JAN	FEB	MAR	APR	MAY	JUN	JUL	AUG	SEP	OCT	NOV	DEC	ANN.
Av. High °F	97	95	90	81	73	67	67	73	81	88	93	96	83
Av. Low °F	70	69	63	54	46	41	39	43	49	58	64	68	55
Humidity	Lo	Lo	Lo	Lo	V.Lo	V.Lo	V.Lo	V.Lo	V.Lo	V.Lo	V.Lo	Lo	V.Lo
Precip. Days	4	3	3	2	2	2	1	2	1	3	4	4	31
Precip. In.	1.7	1.3	1.1	.4	.6	.5	.3	.3	.3	.7	1.2	1.5	9.9
Snowfall In.	0	0	0	0	0	0	0	0	0	0	0	0	0

BRISBANE (QUEENSLAND), AUSTRALIA - 137 ft.

	JAN	FEB	MAR	APR	MAY	JUN	JUL	AUG	SEP	OCT	NOV	DEC	ANN.
Av. High °F	85	85	82	79	74	69	68	71	76	80	82	85	78
Av. Low °F	69	68	66	61	56	51	49	50	55	60	64	67	60
Humidity	Hi	Hi	Hi	Hi	Med	Med	Lo	Lo	Med	Med	Hi	Hi	Med
Precip. Days	13	14	15	12	10	8	8	7	8	9	10	12	126
Precip. In.	6.4	6.3	5.7	3.7	2.8	2.6	2.2	1.9	1.9	2.5	3.7	5.0	44.7
Snowfall In.	0	0	0	0	0	0	0	0	0	0	0	0	0

MELBOURNE (VICTORIA), AUSTRALIA - 115 ft.

	JAN	FEB	MAR	APR	MAY	JUN	JUL	AUG	SEP	OCT	NOV	DEC	ANN.
Av. High °F	78	78	75	68	62	57	56	59	63	67	71	75	67
Av. Low °F	57	57	55	51	47	44	42	43	46	48	51	54	50
Humidity	Med	Med	Med	Med	Lo	Lo	Lo	Lo	Lo	Lo	Med	Med	Med
Precip. Days	9	8	9	13	14	16	17	17	15	14	13	11	156
Precip. In.	1.9	1.8	2.2	2.3	2.1	2.1	1.9	1.9	2.3	2.6	2.3	2.3	25.7
Snowfall In.	0	0	0	0	0	0	0	0	0	0	0	0	0

PERTH (WESTERN AUSTRALIA), AUSTRALIA - 197 ft.

	JAN	FEB	MAR	APR	MAY	JUN	JUL	AUG	SEP	OCT	NOV	DEC	ANN.
Av. High °F	85	85	81	76	69	64	63	64	67	70	76	81	73
Av. Low °F	63	63	61	57	53	50	48	48	50	53	57	61	55
Humidity	Med	Med	Med	Med	Med	Med	Lo	Lo	Lo	Med	Med	Med	Med
Precip. Days	3	3	5	8	15	17	19	19	15	12	7	5	5
Precip. In.	.3	.4	.8	1.7	5.1	7.1	6.7	5.7	3.4	2.2	.8	.5	34.7
Snowfall In.	0	0	0	0	0	0	0	0	0	0	0	0	0

SYDNEY (NEW SOUTH WALES), AUSTRALIA - 138 ft.

	JAN	FEB	MAR	APR	MAY	JUN	JUL	AUG	SEP	OCT	NOV	DEC	ANN.
Av. High °F	78	78	76	71	66	61	60	63	67	71	74	77	70
Av. Low °F	65	65	63	58	52	48	46	48	51	56	60	63	56
Humidity	Hi	Hi	Hi	Med	Lo	Lo	Lo	Lo	Lo	Med	Med	Med	Med
Precip. Days	14	13	14	14	13	12	12	11	12	12	12	13	152
Precip. In.	3.5	4.0	5.0	5.3	5.0	4.6	4.6	3.0	2.9	2.8	2.9	2.9	46.5
Snowfall In.	0	0	0	0	0	0	0	0	0	0	0	0	0

HIGHEST AUSTRALIAN TEMPERATURE: 128°F
Cloncurry, Queensland - January 16, 1889

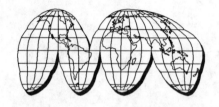

NEW ZEALAND

NEW ZEALAND

Most of New Zealand is farther south, and hence cooler, than most of Australia. In the north, Auckland enjoys a mild climate with frequent rainfall. **Best time to visit** would be *December through March*, although it can get a bit muggy at times.

Wellington is cooler than Auckland. Rainfall here is common, although humidity isn't much of a problem. **Best months to visit** are *January through March*. The winter months can be very wet and chilly.

The climate of the South Island is · quite cool and showery. In spite of these drawbacks the beauty of the area is legendary. Much of the precipitation falls as snow at higher elevations, creating some of the most spectacular Alpine scenery on earth. The climate of Christchurch resembles coastal Washington and Oregon. Temperatures are cool, and rainfall is frequent. The mildest weather occurs from *November through March*.

	JAN	FEB	MAR	APR	MAY	JUN	JUL	AUG	SEP	OCT	NOV	DEC	ANN.
AUCKLAND, NEW ZEALAND - 85 ft.													
Av. High °F	73	73	71	67	62	58	56	58	60	63	66	70	65
Av. Low °F	60	60	59	56	51	48	46	46	49	52	54	57	53
Humidity	Hi	Hi	Med	Med	Med	Lo	Lo	Lo	Lo	Med	Med	Med	Med
Precip. Days	10	10	11	14	19	19	21	19	17	16	15	12	183
Precip. In.	3.1	3.7	3.2	3.8	5.0	5.4	5.7	4.6	4.0	4.0	3.5	3.1	49.1
Snowfall In.	0	0	0	0	0	0	0	0	0	0	0	0	0

HIGHEST ANTARCTICAN TEMPERATURE: 58°F
Esparanza - October 20, 1956

NEW ZEALAND & SOUTH PACIFIC

	JAN	FEB	MAR	APR	MAY	JUN	JUL	AUG	SEP	OCT	NOV	DEC	ANN.
CHRISTCHURCH, NEW ZEALAND - 32 ft.													
Av. High °F	70	69	66	62	56	51	50	52	57	62	66	69	61
Av. Low °F	53	53	50	45	40	36	35	36	40	44	47	51	44
Humidity	Lo	Med	Lo	Lo	Lo	Lo	V.Lo	V.Lo	V.Lo	V.Lo	Lo	Lo	Lo
Precip. Days	10	8	9	10	12	13	13	11	10	10	10	10	126
Precip. In.	2.2	1.7	1.9	1.9	2.6	2.6	2.7	1.9	1.8	1.7	1.9	2.2	25.1
Snowfall In.	0	0	0	0	0	0	0	0	0	0	0	0	0
WELLINGTON, NEW ZEALAND - 415 ft.													
Av. High °F	69	69	67	63	58	55	53	54	57	60	63	67	61
Av. Low °F	56	56	54	51	47	44	42	43	46	48	50	54	49
Humidity	Med	Med	Med	Lo	Lo	Lo	Lo	Lo	Lo	Lo	Lo	Med	Lo
Precip. Days	10	9	11	13	16	17	18	17	15	14	13	12	165
Precip. In.	3.2	3.2	3.2	3.8	4.6	4.6	5.4	4.6	3.8	4.0	3.5	3.5	47.4
Snowfall In.	0	0	0	0	0	0	0	0	0	0	0	0	0

SOUTH PACIFIC

Few areas on Earth can match the beauty of the South Pacific. Tahiti and Fiji lie south of the Equator and hence are warmest and most humid from December through February. The driest months are June through November. The **best month to visit** for moderate temperature, humidity, and the lowest rainfall is *August*.

	JAN	FEB	MAR	APR	MAY	JUN	JUL	AUG	SEP	OCT	NOV	DEC	ANN.
SUVA (FIJI ISLANDS) - 20 ft.													
Av. High °F	86	86	86	84	82	80	79	79	80	81	83	85	83
Av. Low °F	74	74	74	73	71	69	68	68	69	70	71	73	71
Humidity	V.Hi	V.Hi	V.Hi	V.Hi	V.Hi	Hi	Hi	Hi	Hi	Hi	Hi	V.Hi	Hi
Precip. Days	18	18	21	19	16	13	14	15	16	15	15	18	108
Precip. In.	11.4	10.7	14.5	12.2	10.1	6.7	4.9	8.3	7.7	8.3	9.8	12.5	117.1
PAPEETE (TAHITI) - 302 ft.													
Av. High °F	89	89	89	89	87	86	86	86	86	87	88	88	88
Av. Low °F	72	72	72	72	70	69	68	68	69	70	71	72	70
Humidity	V.Hi	V.Hi	V.Hi	V.Hi	V.Hi	V.Hi	V.Hi	V.Hi	V.Hi	V.Hi	V.Hi	V.Hi	V.Hi
Precip. Days	16	16	17	10	10	8	5	6	6	9	13	14	130
Precip. In.	9.9	9.6	6.9	5.6	4.0	3.0	2.1	1.7	2.1	3.5	5.9	9.8	64.1

 # ASTRONOMY

MAJOR METEOR SHOWERS

Shower	Date(s)	Z.H.R.	No. Days
QUADRANTIDS	JAN. 3-4	50-120	0.4
LYRIDS	APR. 22	15- 25	1
ETA AQUARIDS	MAY 4	60	6
S. DELTA AQUARIDS	JUL. 29	30	8
N. DELTA AQUARIDS	AUG. 12	20	8?
PERSEIDS	AUG. 12	60-120	3
ORIONIDS	OCT. 21	30	1.6
SOUTHERN TAURIDS	NOV. 3	15	30?
NORTHERN TAURIDS	NOV. 13	15	30?
LEONIDS	NOV. 17	15	VAR.
GEMINIDS	DEC. 13-14	90	1.5
URSIDS	DEC. 22	15	2

Z.H.R. = ZENITH HOURLY RATE (Number that would be seen per hour by an experienced watcher in a dark sky)

A meteor is a little sand grain or pebble that strikes our atmosphere and burns up. The light during entry is often called a "shooting star". Meteors rarely strike the earth. If they do they are called "meteorites".

Most meteors originate as comets. The nucleus of a comet gradually disintegrates each time it nears the sun. Particles are shed by this nucleus and continue travelling in the same orbit. Eventually, some of these particles spread out along the comet's path. If the path of the Earth crosses this stream of particles we experience a meteor shower.

All meteors of a shower arrive from the same direction at the same speed. Therefore, they seem to come from the same part of the sky (called its radiant) A shower is named for the constellation from which it radiates.

Over thousands of years, a meteor stream will gradually disperse due to the gravitational pull of the planets. The shower will then become "diffuse" - the number of meteors declines, and the shower spreads out over weeks instead of hours or days. A meteor that doesn't belong to a shower is called "sporadic".

While in space, particles are called meteoroids. When one strikes the atmosphere it is called a meteor with its brief streak of light. A very bright meteor is called a "fireball". An exploding meteor is called a "bolide". Some of the brightest ones leave glowing "trains" of luminous smoke.

A meteor's brightness depends on its size, speed, composition and the angle at which it hits the atmosphere. A "fireball" may start out as a particle that weighs only an ounce.

More meteors can be seen in the hours just before dawn.

SOLAR ECLIPSES

July 22, 1990 - Total eclipse can be seen over Finland and Northeastern U.S.S.R. Partial eclipse covers most of Europe, U.S.S.R., N. Asia, N. Japan, Alaska, W. & Central Canada, Pacific Northwest, and south to Southern California.

July 11, 1991 - Total eclipse over S. Baja California, S. Mexico, and Hawaii. Partial eclipse covers most of N. and S. America.

LUNAR ECLIPSES

August 6, 1990 - Partial eclipse visible over California, S. Alaska, E. Siberia, S.E. Asia, Australia and New Zealand.

December 9, 1992 - Total eclipse can be seen over most of the world.

INDEX OF U.S. CITIES

INDEX OF WORLD CITIES

INDEX OF WORLD COUNTRIES

99

To Order Additional Copies Of The International Traveler's Weather Guide

Book Rates

1 to 4 books = $9.95 per book

5 to 10 books = $8.95 per book

11 to 24 books = $7.95 per book

25 or more books = $6.95 per book

* Prices includes postage and handling. *

Send check or money order to: (Price includes book, postage and handling.)

Weather Press
2443 Fair Oaks Blvd.
Suite #330G
Sacramento, CA 95825

Total books _____ at $9.95 each (or see scale). Enclosed is $ _____
Make payable to *Weather Press*.

Name: _____

Address: _____

City: _____ State: _____ Zip: _____

Please allow 3 to 4 weeks for delivery.